THE DISSOLUTION OF
THE MONASTERIES

BLANDFORD HISTORY SERIES

(General Editor: R. W. Harris)

The Dissolution of the Monasteries

G. W. O. WOODWARD

Professor of History
University of Canterbury,
Christchurch, New Zealand

BLANDFORD PRESS
LONDON

First published in 1966
2nd impression 1969
© 1966 Blandford Press Ltd,
167 High Holborn, London W.C.1

SBN 7137 0422 5

*Set in 11pt Times, Printed in Great Britain by
Richard Clay (The Chaucer Press), Ltd.,
Bungay, Suffolk*

CONTENTS

SECTION III:

THE AFTERMATH

Acknowledgments

THE author wishes to acknowledge with gratitude his indebtedness to the following persons and societies for permission to reproduce the material utilised in the appendices of documents:—

Miss E. M. Walker, F.S.A., and the Council of the Yorkshire Archaeological Society (Chapters 1 and 6); Miss K. Major, M.A., B.Litt., F.S.A., and the Lincoln Record Society (Chapter 2); Mrs. N. K. M. Gurney, M.A., and the Borthwick Institute of Historical Research (Chapters 3 and 10); The Keeper of the Public Records (Chapters 6 and 9); Mr. W. R. Ward, M.A., D.Phil., and the Chetham Society (Chapter 7); Professor H. S. Offler, M.A., and the Surtees Society (Chapter 10).

Acknowledgments are due for photographs reproduced, as follows:

Aerofilms and Aero Pictorial Ltd.: Illustrations Nos. 1, 2, 7, 8, 10.

Victoria & Albert Museum: Illustrations Nos. 4, 11, 12.

Public Record Office: Illustrations Nos. 3 (E.344/21/3 fol. 14), 5 (S.P.5/2, fol. 6) and 6 (S.P.5/2, fol. 1).

Director in Aerial Photography, University of Cambridge: Illustration No. 9. This is Crown Copyright.

List of Illustrations

Section I

The Place of the Religious Orders in Society

1

The Monasteries as Property Owners

NOWADAYS, unless we happen to live in the immediate vicinity of some famous monastery, or to take a personal interest in the life and work of the religious orders, we are unlikely to be very much aware of their existence, let alone to have any very clear ideas about the nature and value of the monastic discipline, or any real acquaintance with the men and women who have dedicated themselves to it. We do not often see monks, nuns or friars wearing their distinctive habits in our streets. We may have encountered them occasionally on our sightseeing trips to Caldey, Buckfast or Mount St. Bernard, but they are hardly part of our daily experience. It is difficult for us, therefore, fully to appreciate how extensive and important was the share of the religious orders in the daily life of our country in the years before the dissolution of the monasteries in the reign of Henry VIII when they almost certainly numbered in their ranks a very much greater proportion of the population than they do today. In 1530, only a few years before the dissolution, there were at least 825 religious houses in England and Wales (502 monasteries of all kinds, 136 nunneries and 187 friaries) which between them housed something like 7,500 men and 1,800 women, making a total of around 9,300 religious persons out of a population which was probably not much more than $3\frac{1}{2}$ million. The proportion of religious persons to the total population was therefore about 1 to 375. There were few parts of the country where monks and nuns were not to be found; they were a very familiar part of daily life for many people.

The Wealth of the Monasteries

But the importance of the monastic orders in the days before the dissolution is not to be measured in numbers alone. We must also remember that in an age when landowning was the principal form of wealth the religious orders were landlords on a very large scale. Just how extensive were their estates it is not now possible to say with any real degree of accuracy. All the estimates which from time to time have been made of the proportion of the wealth of the nation which was in the possession of the monks and nuns, or of the acreage of their lands, have involved at some stage of the calculation the making of assumptions which are so ill-founded in demonstrable fact as to deprive the final figure of most of its value. Such information as we do possess is insufficient to enable us to do more than make an informed guess at the answer. We do know, for example, with a fair degree of certainty, that the total annual income of all the religious orders was, in 1535, in the region of £160,000 to £200,000; but, as we have no means of ascertaining what the total national income was at that time, we are unable to make any comparison save on the basis of an arbitrary estimate of the latter figure. Nor do we get much further if we try to convert monastic income into acreage and to express the result as a proportion of the total land area of the kingdom, for such a calculation involves us in the need to determine what was the average income per acre of monastic estates, and this varied so much from district to district and according to the use to which the land was put (pasture, ploughland, meadow, woodland, etc.) that any national average can again be little more than an arbitrary estimate.

These difficulties have not, however, inhibited writers in the past. Simon Fish, the anti-clerical author of *A Supplication for the Beggars* which first appeared in 1529, declared roundly that the clergy 'have gotten into their hands more than the third part of' the kingdom, though he did not indicate how he had arrived at that figure. We need not be surprised at this absence of proof in a propaganda pamphlet of this kind, but what is very surprising is the way in which this rough and ready figure of one-third has been taken up and repeated by so many subsequent writers, some of whom have even taken Fish's statement to refer to the wealth of the religious orders alone, whereas he clearly had in mind the *whole* of the clergy 'bishops, abbots, priors, deacons, archdeacons, suffragans, priests, monks, canons, friars, pardoners and summoners.'

Even Fish would hardly have claimed for the monastic orders very much more than a half share in that third of the kingdom which he would have us believe the church as a whole possessed.

Other estimates of the wealth of the religious orders are as varied as their authors' backgrounds and intentions. One enterprising, but anonymous, writer in 1717, after an elaborate calculation based upon sixteenth-century figures for monastic income and land-tax figures for his own day, came to the remarkable conclusion that as much as seven-tenths of the land of the kingdom had once been in the possession of the monasteries! But this is the extreme case. Other estimates are more moderate, ranging from one-sixth to one-twentieth.

Secular and Spiritual Lordships

And yet, even if all these general estimates, for the reasons given above, must be treated with a great deal of reserve, we can still make use of other and more limited comparisons to help us to understand how important was the share of the monastic orders in the national economy. In 1410 a petition presented in parliament claimed that the landed possessions of the bishops and abbeys, if applied to secular purposes, would suffice to maintain 15 earls, 1,500 knights and 6,200 squires in the style of living appropriate to their rank, would provide, in addition, for the maintenance of 100 alms-houses, and would yet leave £20,000 a year in the hands of the king. The figures given in this petition need not be taken any more seriously than those given by Simon Fish. They are not meant to be precise. They are little more than round sums used dramatically to establish that the church was very wealthy. And yet, the analogy drawn between great earldoms and great abbeys, between knights and more modest priories, between secular and religious establishments in general, is a useful one, and one that would come naturally to men in the sixteenth and well as in the fifteenth century. The earl, or great nobleman, with his family, retainers, servants and dependants to maintain in his great mansion on the proceeds of an income derived mainly from land, had his natural ecclesiastical counterpart in the great abbot with his monks, servants and equally elaborate household, also dependent upon the proceeds of an almost exclusively landed income. If we accept this analogy and think of the abbeys as lordships in ecclesiastical hands, regarding the religious orders as a sub-division of the landed class rather than as a separate social or economic group, we should, by making a few comparisons, be able to get a better idea of the importance of the monasteries in their own day.

The petitioners of 1410 assumed, for the purpose of their calculations, that an earl should have an income of at least £2,000 a year. A century and more later, in the 1530s, when so many of the greater noble estates had, by reason of the forfeitures and counter-forfeitures of the intervening years, passed into the hands of the crown, an income of £2,000 was probably rather more than most earls could boast of. In the early years of the reign of Henry VIII, for example, the earl of Northumberland was spending around £1,000 a year in maintaining his extensive household of 166 persons. His total income was probably in excess of this figure, but is unlikely to have reached the £2,000 mark. On the other hand, in 1535 the five wealthiest religious houses in the country (Glastonbury, Canterbury cathedral, Westminster, St. Albans and the house of the Knights of St. John in Clerkenwell) were all reckoned to be worth more than £2,000 a year and were, therefore, by the criterion of 1410, worthy to rank with earls. A further nineteen great abbeys were in the same year valued at more than £1,000 a year, so that it is clear that these major houses did form something of a religious aristocracy, as wealthy and as influential in society as any of the greater nobles.

Farther down the social scale, the middle range of abbeys, with incomes between £200 and £700, of which there were nearly 150, were certainly worth in terms of wealth and social influence as much as several knights apiece. Even the humblest priories, with only £20 or £30 a year to their name, can be thought of as the social equivalents of the lesser gentry. Though we may be unwilling to follow the petitioners of 1410 in suggesting any exact secular equivalent (in terms of peers, knights and gentry) of the possessions of more than eight hundred religious houses of very varied size and fortune, we should be safe in assuming that their share of the landed wealth of the kingdom was very considerable indeed, and that the dissolution of the religious orders entailed the transfer to the crown of property far in excess, in value and extent, of any that had ever previously been acquired by a single act of forfeiture or resumption.

It is not, however, only in terms of the size and sources of their income that the religious orders may be regarded as the ecclesiastical

B

equivalents of secular nobles and gentry. The social position which the abbeys enjoyed as a consequence of their wealth and estates carried with it definite responsibilities which the abbots and priors were expected to discharge in very much the same way as any other landowner.

Abbots in Parliament

In the first place the heads of thirty important abbeys and priories were Lords of Parliament, and were accustomed to receive individual writs of summons whenever parliament met. Among those who enjoyed this privilege were the heads of the five wealthiest houses already named, but some of the other parliamentary abbots came from houses of rather more modest means so that it was not simply a case of the wealthiest religious corporations having the monopoly of this right of direct representation in parliament. Together with the twenty-one English and Welsh bishops the parliamentary abbots made up the number of the Lords Spiritual, who, had they all been present, could have formed a very substantial group, indeed an actual majority, in the upper house, for, at the beginning of the reign of Henry VIII there were only about forty lay peers. It is interesting, however, to notice that, whatever the historical origins of this representation of the clergy in parliament, the judges in 1515 declared that the Lords Spiritual

'have no place in the Parliament-chamber by reason of their spirituality, but only by reason of their temporal possessions'.

In other words it was their estates, their social position and not their ecclesiastical which secured for the bishops and abbots their entry to parliament, and once there they did not form a separate estate or house, but remained on a par with the Lords Temporal, their fellow landlords. In this judicial pronouncement we can therefore see very clearly that assimilation of ecclesiastical to secular lordship, that tendency to regard the religious houses as little more than lordships in ecclesiastical hands, which we have already remarked upon.

It must not be thought, however, that the abbots, despite their numbers, played any very significant part in the deliberations of parliament. The abbot of Westminster, whose chapter house was for many years used by the Commons as their meeting place, was, as might be expected, a very regular attender. So was the abbot of

Waltham, a house much favoured by Henry VIII. Colchester, Reading, St. Albans and Abingdon also have a good attendance record. But many abbots were, by the standards of their day, already elderly men when they took office. Parliaments were more often than not held in the winter season when the roads were bad and travelling was difficult. It is not surprising, therefore, to find that the attendance record of some of the abbots from the more distant parts of the kingdom was not very good. The journals of the House of Lords reveal that in the earlier years of the reign of Henry VIII there were seldom more than ten abbots present in parliament at any one time. The few letters of excuse for absence which survive all tell much the same story; the abbot is old and infirm, and the trials of the journey to Westminster would be too much for him to undertake. On the other hand, those abbots who did attend parliament fairly regularly do not seem to have offered at any point any very effective resistance to the passage of the 'reformation' statutes in the 1530s. Even the act of 1536 for the dissolution of the lesser monasteries seems to have received their ready approbation, though it may be, as the chronicler Edward Hall suggests, that they gave their consent

'in the hope that their great monasteries should have continued still.'

Abbots as Commissioners

Service in parliament was the privilege, and the duty, of a select group of abbots who found themselves expected to play their part in the affairs of state in much the same way as any contemporary secular lord. But others besides the parliamentary abbots also found themselves caught up in the machinery of government. In common with other substantial subjects throughout the kingdom the heads of the principal abbeys and priories were expected to perform, on behalf of the crown, many of the tasks of government, both routine and otherwise. In some shires, for example, you will find one or two abbots being appointed as justices of the peace. In this capacity they had a multitude of duties to perform, not only were they responsible for petty criminal jurisdiction and the maintenance of the peace, but the oversight of local government was also in their hands. They joined with their fellow justices in supervising the repair of highways and bridges, and the licensing of ale houses. They reported to the king's council any untoward happenings or suspicious characters in their area. They carried out to the best of their ability virtually any task that the government chose to impose upon them.

Frequently, for the discharge of special tasks, additional commissions were issued, and on the *ad hoc* bodies thus created abbots are often found at work. In the fenland area the task of supervising the maintenance and repair of the all-important land drainage system was entrusted to commissioners for sewers, among whom were regularly numbered the abbots of Crowland, Revesby, Bardney and Kirkstead and the prior of Spalding. The abbot of Battle shared a like responsibility in the low-lying parts of Sussex; the abbots of Westminster and St. Augustine's Canterbury in the Thames estuary; and the abbot of Meaux in Holderness. In 1513 when England and Scotland were at war and commissioners were appointed to seek out and seize the goods of enemy aliens, abbots were among those named in nearly every shire to adjudicate in any disputes that might arise out of such seizures. In 1528, a year of dearth, the abbot of Jervaulx in Yorkshire was commissioned with others to search for hoarded grains. Many other instances could be cited, but it should be clear from those already quoted that, in appointing agents for the discharge of the great variety of tasks which it delegated to commissioners, the government drew no real distinction between the heads of religious houses and the local nobility and gentry. All enjoyed a similar social status and as a consequence were expected to perform the same type of services. It should also be clear that the performance of such secular and inescapable duties must perforce have diverted some of the energies of the abbots concerned away from their strictly spiritual responsibilities and made them of necessity men of affairs. Indeed some, such as the abbot of York, whose abbey served for many years before its dissolution as the depository for a royal treasury for the defence of the north, were so continuously concerned with governmental business that they could have had but little time for the affairs of their own houses, and even less for the pursuit of the monastic life.

Property and Litigation

But it was not only the government and its business which demanded of certain abbots a considerable proportion of their time and energies. As the heads of propertied corporations in a highly litigious age they also found themselves obliged quite frequently to engage in private law suits in defence of the possessions and rights of their houses. In this respect also there was little to distinguish the religious orders from their secular contemporaries among the landed classes. The records of the law courts feature the names and claims of religious houses with the greatest regularity, and not always in a favourable light. Of course in many instances the monks or nuns are merely concerned to defend their properties and endowments from the greedy grasp of avaricious neighbours. In an age still recovering from the comparative lawlessness of the mid-fifteenth century few landowners could altogether avoid engaging in litigation if they wished to survive, and cases of trespass and disputes over land titles and the terms of leases are very frequent and reflect, for the most part, no particular credit or discredit upon the religious persons and houses involved. But there are also cases in which the heads of religious houses are accused of highly discreditable activities, a well-documented, if rather extreme, example being provided by John Hexham, the penultimate abbot of Whitby. Secure in the comparative isolation of the north-east Yorkshire coast, and in the strength of the cliff-top position of his house, he seems to have lorded it over the surrounding district in a truly high-handed manner. Even his election to the abbacy in 1527 was effected in circumstances which gave rise to the suspicion that undue pressures had been brought to bear. Then, as abbot, we find him interfering arbitrarily in the affairs of monastic tenants, engaged in a riotous contest with the mariners of the town, and working in league with French pirates. And yet he remained abbot until 1538 when he resigned, apparently voluntarily, on the score of ill health.

Few abbots had careers quite as colourful as that of Hexham, but he was by no means the only one of his contemporaries to appear in the legal records of his time in a bad light. Another Yorkshire abbot, Marmaduke Huby of Fountains, who had an excellent reputation among his fellow Cistercians as an efficient and energetic administrator, an ambitious builder, and a tireless visitor and reformer, is nevertheless found as one of the defendants in a Star Chamber action in which he is accused of conspiring to defeat the course of justice. A certain Miles Willesthorpe complains that the abbot and others have combined together to deprive him of legal redress for the damages he has sustained at the hands of

'persons unlawfully stirred by the procurement and assistance of the said confederates and by their several commandments'.

His cousin has been ambushed and sorely beaten. The fence enclosing his park has been pulled down on at least five occasions and the game therein hunted. A house belonging to him and a water mill have been destroyed, his orchards and woods felled, and his millpond drained and fished. And yet all his attempts to secure justice have been defeated by the 'said confederacy and embracement' of the abbot and his fellow defendants. Even an earlier appeal to the king's council has proved ineffective, for, although he had obtained letters under the Privy Seal summoning the offending parties to appear in the Star Chamber, the attempt of his servant to deliver these had provoked further assaults and a crop of vexatious law suits. However, in this case, as in so many others, we do not know the outcome. Only the very detailed bill of complaint and the brief denials of two of the lesser defendants have been preserved, and we must hesitate to confuse accusation with condemnation. Nevertheless it remains significant that, whether abbot Huby was or was not as deeply involved as Willesthorpe alleged he was, the complainant should have been prepared to believe that an abbot was as likely to be guilty of embracery and the other crimes of 'overmighty subjects' as any other great landowner. A similar, but briefer, complaint against the abbot of Rievaulx is quoted in the appendix to this chapter. The records of the courts of law reveal almost no distinction between the behaviour of monastic landlords and that of their secular equivalents.

Estate Management

In the management of their estates there is also practically no distinction to be drawn between monastic and lay landlords. The romantic notion that the monks were somehow 'good' or 'old-fashioned' landlords when compared with the rapacious and ruthlessly efficient laymen who took over the monastic estates after the dissolution, is not easily sustained by the evidence available. The economic pressures which obliged the secular landlords in the sixteenth century to overhaul the management of their estates, to raise rents and to renew leases on terms less favourable to the tenants, operated equally forcibly upon the monks, particularly in the last two decades before the dissolution. Rising costs, resulting from the general price rise, compelled those monks who wished to maintain their accustomed style of living to find additional sources of income. The days when they could look to pious patrons to increase their endowments were past. The founding of chantries and of schools was now the fashionable outlet for those who wished to perform some act of piety on their deathbed. Gifts to the older established religious houses were rare and generally small. The foundation of new ones, such as the Greenwich house of Franciscan Observants established by Edward IV, was exceptional. If more money was needed it could only be found by raising rents and increasing admission fines. The religious orders could no more afford the luxury of being 'easy land-lords' than could any secular landlord caught in the inflationary spiral of the sixteenth century. And so we must not be surprised to find John Alanbrigge, last abbot of Byland, suddenly demanding from one of his tenants a 'gressom', or admission fine for the renewal of a lease, equal to two years' instead of the customary three months' rent. Nor should we think it strange to read of monastic tenants having their rents increased, or even of their being evicted like a certain aged couple, Thomas and Alice Brown, he deaf, lame and blind, and she frightened almost out of her mind by the threatenings of the abbot who was their landlord and wanted to give their holding to a kinsman of his own. Other abbots are to be found taking the initiative in projects for the enclosure and improvement of land, once again in order to keep pace with the rising cost of living.

Of course the fact that the larger abbeys commonly employed the assistance of numerous laymen in the administration of their pro-perties must have helped to minimise any difference there might otherwise have been between the running of monastic and secular estates. Every great abbey had its staff of stewards, receivers and bailiffs, many of them neighbouring gentry and landowners in their own right, whose advice to their monastic employers would naturally be coloured by their own experience in the management of their own lands. Secular and monastic estate management would naturally tend to run on similar lines when the same persons were involved in both.

The Monks as Managers

And yet two words of caution must be uttered at this point. In the first place, though the monks employed lay administrative assistance quite extensively this did not necessarily mean that they abdicated all control over their affairs to the laity and took no personal part in the management of their own estates. Enough examples are on record to show that even at some of the greatest monasteries with the largest lay staffs the brethren themselves took a close and active interest in matters of business. At St. Mary's in York, despite the large body of laymen employed, it was one of the monks, Richard Watson, who filled the key administrative office of 'Master of the Manors'. In this capacity he was concerned with many aspects of the affairs of most of the abbey's properties. One of these was the little fishing port of Hornsea on the North Sea coast. When the harbour there was in need of repair the responsibility fell upon the monks as lords of the manor, and when the repair work was put in hand in about 1537 it was not one of the many lay officials and servants of the monastery, but Watson himself who went down to Hornsea at regular intervals over a period of two years or so, to pay the workmen and to supervise the work in hand.

At another Yorkshire house, the Cistercian abbey of Roche, John Dodsworth, one of the senior monks who held the office of bursar, was accustomed to go twice weekly in harvest time to the neighbouring town of Tickhill to supervise in person the gathering in of the abbey's tithe sheaves. At nearby Monk Bretton the monks employed a lay steward to hold their annual court in neighbouring Cudworth, but one of the monks went with him to see how he discharged his stewardship. The monks at these houses, and at others too, did not sit back and let their lay assistants manage things for them. They were themselves men of affairs.

The second word of caution is a *caveat* to the effect that the statement that the religious houses employed lay assistance extensively is true only of the greater abbeys. Indeed almost every statement that we care to make about the large, wealthy and well-known religious houses must be qualified by the warning that what we say about them will very probably not be true of the many very small, very poor and very obscure convents, mostly nunneries, which are found at the other end of the scale. Against the five greatest monasteries which, as we have already noticed, enjoyed an income of over £2,000 a year we must set the eighty-seven which had £30 or less. The nineteen with incomes between £1,000 and £2,000 are more than balanced by the forty-nine which had between £30 and £50. These smaller priories, it is true, did, like their larger and more famous counterparts, derive their income chiefly from land, but few of them possessed much more than their demesnes in the immediate vicinity which they farmed themselves with the minimum of lay assistance. Most of them did manage to secure the services of some local noble or gentleman as chief steward in return for a small annual fee, but the chief steward was not normally required to take an active interest in the daily administration of the affairs of the house. His function was to look after the interests of the abbey or priory in the world at large, and to use his influence on its behalf at court or wherever else need should arise. Apart from a chief steward a small priory might quite frequently employ a receiver or an auditor if there were rents from outlying properties to be collected, but few of the really small houses employed any more lay assistance than this. Some did not even rise to this minimum establishment and had to be their own managers and accountants.

Even where lay administrative assistance was employed it was still sometimes necessary for the religious in the smaller houses to play a very active and personal part in the running of their affairs. The little Benedictine nunnery of Moxby was valued in 1535 at £26 a year. It employed the services of two stewards and a bailiff, but this did not mean that the nuns were freed entirely from secular cares. In later years they remembered the delights of haymaking and harvest, and two of them were able to relate how 'amongst other young nuns of the nunnery' they 'helped to do such necessary business as was to be done' and in particular 'helped in hay time to make the hay', one of them making up stooks and the other 'raking after the wains that led away the hay'. Many another small convent must have been run in much the same way, for with so small an endowment there was little to spare for the wages of employees, and most houses of this size had only three or four hands on their payroll in addition to five or six domestic servants. The contrast with the larger abbeys where twenty or thirty stewards, receivers and bailiffs would be employed in supervising the outlying properties of the abbey, and well over a hundred domestics and field hands kept busy about the house and its demesnes, hardly needs to be emphasised.

APPENDIX: A STAR CHAMBER PLEA

Walter Percehay *v* the Abbot and Bursar of Rievaulx, 1519.

(From Yorkshire Star Chamber Proceedings, vol. II, no. LXIX, Yorkshire Archaeological Society's Record Series, vol. XLV, pp. 180–1. Percehay complains to Wolsey as Lord Chancellor that he has been forcibly and unjustly deprived of his right to dig turves on the moors near Pickering, and that, because of the power and local influence of the abbot, he has no hope of securing redress at common law. This is by no means an exceptional case. It should be noticed, however, that what we have here is only the initial bill of complaint. The answers of the defendants are not extant, nor do we know the outcome of the case. We should therefore reserve our judgment. The spelling in this extract has been modernised, with the exception of the surnames which have been left as in the original.)

To the most reverend father in God, Thomas, lord cardinal, archbishop of York, and Chancellor of England.

Meekly beseecheth your gracious lordship your humble orator Walter Percehay of Ryton in the county of York, gentleman, that where your said orator and all other his ancestors hath ever used and had time out of mind of man, in peaceable manner without interruption or impediment of any person or persons, as well common of pasture as of estovers of and upon the waste ground and common called the moors at Pickering, and in all the forests within the county of York, as the digging of turves in the waste ground and common for the expenses of your said orator according to the custom of that country used, that is to say the pasture of the said waste ground for his cattle and beasts without number, as to have and take of and upon the same common sufficient firebote, hedgebote, ploughbote, cartbote, gatebote and housebote for the necessary expenses to be spent within and about his tenants' houses and lands, for the reparations and buildings of the same adjoining to the said common, so it is now, most gracious lord, that Dan. William Scarburgh, being bursar of the house and monastery of Rievaulx, within the said county of York, Robert Norham the elder, John Spenlay, Bryan Wodecok, William Adhams, John Hogger, John Nokes, Christopher Pynder, Thomas Pole, Charles Pole, Thomas Bugge, William Norham, John Norham, Robert Norham the younger, Thomas Baillan, Edmund Pynder, Thomas Woodde, John Walker, John Bowys, and Thomas Chapman, being tenants and servants unto William abbot of the said house and monastery of Rievaulx, pretending to disherit your said orator of his said right in the said common, by the assent and commandment of the said abbot the foresaid persons, with divers other persons to the number of 30 and above, whose names be to your said orator unknown, the 20th day of June, the 11th year of our sovereign lord the King that now is, with force and arms in riotous manner, that is to say with staves, swords, bucklers and weapons, contrary to the King's peace and laws, at Pickering aforesaid assembled themselves, and with like riot, force and arms, having there 7 wains, carried away the turves of your said orator which he had afore caused to be digged in the common called Mares Moors, in Pickering aforesaid, to his great costs and charges, against all right and good conscience, took away, and forasmuch as the said abbot, being a man of great possessions and of power within the said county, intending utterly to destroy and take away from your said orator his said common of pasture and of estovers, your said orator being a poor gentleman and is not able to sue for his right after the course of the common law against the said abbot and his servants, by reason whereof he is like to be put from his right in the said common, unless your gracious goodness be to him showed in this behalf. In consideration whereof it may please your gracious lordship, the premises considered, to grant to your said orator the King's letters of privy seal as well against the said abbot and Dan. William Scarburgh with other riotous persons aforesaid, commanding them and every of them to appear afore your gracious lordship in the Star Chamber at Westminster, at a certain day and under a certain pain by your grace to be limited, they and every of them there to answer to the premises for the love of God and in the way of charity.

per me Humphrey Broun.

2

The Cloister and the Community

ENOUGH should now have been said to make it quite clear that the monastic orders had of necessity, as a consequence of their position as property owners, to live very much in the world and to concern themselves with worldly affairs, with rents, leases, litigation, local government, and matters of state. But it was not to engage in such activities that the monasteries and nunneries had first been founded. Time and circumstance may have compelled the monks and nuns to be thus worldly-wise in defence of their endowments, and their contemporaries were sometimes quick to criticise them if they failed to show a proper concern for the rights and properties of which they were for the time being the possessors, but those same endowments had originally been given to them to enable them the better to lead an unworldly life devoted to prayer and worship. This was the original, and always the most important, function of the religious orders, and one which our secular-minded century is inclined to belittle or to overlook. The keeping of schools; the housing of travellers; the maintenance of the poor; the tending of the infirm; however beneficial such works may have been to the community at large they were at all times secondary to the great duty of maintaining the daily round of prayer and praise which was made up by the monastic hours, and of celebrating the regular sequence of intercessory masses for the souls of deceased benefactors. Thomas Fuller, the seventeenth century historian of the English church, writing for a generation of Englishmen who lived more than a century after the dissolution, has some nice phrases to describe the monasteries; 'Magazines of merit' for the founder, his ancestors and posterity; or again

'Corporations of prayers, twisted cables to draw down blessings on their
patrons' heads'.

Slightly mocking though Fuller's tone may be, he has the right idea
about the prime function of monastic houses. Those who roundly
assert that in the early part of the sixteenth century the monasteries
and nunneries no longer fulfilled any useful function in society are
entitled to their opinion, but too often are inclined to condemn the
religious orders for failing in their secondary functions without
enquiring very closely whether they were in fact still fulfilling their
prime one. In point of fact the evidence on this last point is capable of
bearing rather divergent interpretations.

Prayer

All houses of religion which had not at some time, either individually,
or as members of particular orders, secured from the papacy exemption from the jurisdiction of the local diocesan bishop were subject
to periodic visitation by that bishop or by deputies acting in his name.
A visitation was a solemn and formidable occasion when the bishop
or his representative sat in state in the chapter house of the abbey,
summoned each member of the community before him in turn, and
interrogated them individually about every aspect of the common life
from the manner in which divine service was carried out to the quality
of the food supplied from the kitchens. Now the surviving records of
such visitations do make it quite clear that the visitors continued,
right down to the last days of monasticism in England, to pay particular attention to the way in which the various church services were
performed. This prime function of the religious orders was certainly
not neglected. But how faithfully the monks and nuns maintained the
full cycle of the eight daily offices and the daily masses besides, it is
not easy to say. We do know that in some cases discipline was rather
lax. At Wymondham (Norfolk) in 1492 it was reported to the visitor
that the monks recited the offices *morose*, in a miserable manner.
At Woodbridge (Suffolk) in 1520 they sang the psalms neither dis-
tinctly nor yet with devotion. At St. Mary of Carrow (Norwich) in
1526 the nuns chanted too quickly. At Goring (Oxfordshire) in 1530,
only one nun was capable of leading the choir.

None of these faults is very serious, and echoes of them all can
be heard in many a parish church today, but at Stainfield (Lincs.) in

1519 a rather more serious accusation was made, namely that some nuns did not sing in the choir, but slept in their stalls instead. Others at that same house sat up too late in the evening and then did not rise for matins in the night. This last complaint, of laxity in attending the night office, is that most commonly recorded in the two sets of printed visitation records from which so much of our knowledge of the quality of sixteenth-century monastic life is drawn. The *Visitations in the Diocese of Lincoln* (Lincoln Record Society vols. 35 and 37) contain parts of the record of 102 visits to sixty-four monastic houses in the years between 1517 and 1531. There are twenty occasions when slackness in observing the daily round of services is noted by the visitor, and on eleven of these occasions the complaint is that not all the community rise regularly for matins. The picture presented by the *Norwich Visitations* (Camden Society, N.S. XLIII) is very similar. In this diocese the records cover 136 visits to thirty-six houses between 1492 and 1532. There are eighteen complaints about slackness in attendance at services, of which seven are of failures to rise for matins.

But what do these figures mean? Can we be sure that the bishop and his officers discovered and corrected all cases of slack observance? How many went undetected? If the monks or nuns did not themselves raise the matter with the visitor he had no sure means of knowing how faithful they were to their duty. Was laxity a common fault only occasionally detected, or an uncommon one rigorously corrected wherever it was observed? The surviving records will bear either interpretation, depending chiefly upon how efficient we consider episcopal visitation was as a means of maintaining discipline, and that must remain largely a matter of opinion.

Schools

On the subject of the more tangible social services provided by the religious orders, the printed visitation records are not very illuminating. There is, for example, only one reference, and that an ambiguous one, to a monastic school-house (at Bromehill, Norfolk, in 1514) which was then in need of repair, but nothing else to indicate directly that any religious house kept a school. It is true that the bishop or his representative quite frequently noted on visitation that there was no schoolmaster at a particular abbey, and gave orders that one should be appointed. But so often it is specifically stated that this man's task was to instruct the novices or the junior monks in 'grammar' that it is difficult not to accept the conclusion that, even where his duties were not thus specified, the *magister grammaticalis* in a religious house was concerned exclusively with the education of those within the order or those about to enter it, and that his presence there is no evidence that the monks kept a school for the benefit of the neighbouring people. Even where we find references to the presence of boys or children in a religious house we must not jump to the conclusion that they were attending school there. Many of the larger abbeys maintained boy choristers who received their keep and some instruction (mainly in reading and singing) in return for their services in the choir. The boys at Leicester who, it was complained in 1518, gave themselves over to sports and hunting, and those at Norwich whose numbers had in 1520 fallen from the proper total of fourteen to eight, were almost certainly choristers, as were undoubtedly the 'fourteen children for the chapel' at Ulverscroft in Charnwood. Less certain is the role of the children at Burnham nunnery (Bucks.) for whose keep, it was alleged in 1521, no proper provision was made, or of those at Catesby (Northants.) who played in the cloister and sat in the choir and, presumably, broke the accustomed silence of the house. Were they choristers, young scholars or just the local children at their play?

On the whole the contribution of the religious orders to education was not very significant. The medieval grammar schools, some of them permanently endowed by fourteenth or fifteenth-century benefactors, others still largely dependent upon the fees of pupils, were for the most part independent of the monasteries. Occasionally, as at Evesham or Winchcombe, the monks might be required to provide from their revenues a salary for the schoolmaster in charge of the local grammar school, but in such cases the religious were rather the trustees of the estate of the school founder than the actual providers of the school. At other places, such as Sherbourne, a religious house might be under an obligation to provide scholarships to the local grammar school for a certain number of boys, thus helping them to acquire learning without dispensing it directly.

There are, at best, only a few references here and there which suggest that some monasteries did keep schools of their own which were attended by others besides junior monks, novices and choristers. At West Acre (Norfolk) it was, for example, observed in 1520 that there was no one appointed to teach 'the brethren and the boys'. Of course the 'boys' might just be choristers, or young novices, but they might also be a younger generation of those sons of the gentry whom an earlier visitor, in 1494, had noted frequenting that self-same priory, though nothing, it was then complained, was paid for their board. Why should the sons of the gentry have frequented West Acre unless to acquire an education of some sort? At Thetford nunnery in 1532 it was, in rather similar fashion, a cause of complaint that a certain John Jerves had sent his daughter to dwell in the house but had paid nothing towards her keep. Was this a case of unpaid school-fees? It might well be. But even if there were schools at West Acre and Thetford, they were exceptions to the general rule that such schooling as was provided by the religious orders was exclusively for the benefit of the inhabitants of the cloister itself. No widespread national educational disaster was likely to follow if the monasteries were dissolved.

Hospitality

The offering of shelter and food to travellers was a duty which devolved upon others besides the monks, for the social custom of the day required that every man of substance should provide hospitality for the wayfarer, and it was a point of pride among the gentry and nobility that they should be famed for the generosity of their house and table. Yet it was chiefly to the monasteries that the traveller turned, and we know from the ruins which survive that even the humblest convent had its *hospitium* or guest house where the passer-by could secure a meal and a place to sleep. The quality of such hospitality must have varied as much as that provided by modern inns. A lot would depend upon the number of visitors entertained and the wealth or poverty of the house itself. No specific charges were made, but the well-to-do guest was expected to make a suitable offering when leaving.

There is no evidence of any general falling off in the standards of monastic hospitality in the early sixteenth century. There were some complaints, of course, about declining standards at some houses, as at Ramsey (Hunts.) in 1518, or at Campsey nunnery (Suffolk) where, in 1532, the gentlefolk who visited the house were complaining of the meanness of the prioress. The nuns at the latter house were also complaining at that time about the poor quality of the food and the lateness of their meals, so the guests had no cause to feel that they were being deliberately victimised. On the other hand, at Stainfield (Lincs.) in 1519 the quality of the hospitality was so good that the bishop had to issue orders that no visitor was to be allowed to stay for more than a few days. Pilgrims passing through Crowland on their way to Walsingham encountered an unusual hazard, a perverse gatekeeper who deliberately set them on the wrong road, but, on the other hand, 'the King's subjects and strangers travelling the seas' received 'great relief and comfort' at the hands of the monks of Netley (Hampshire) and Quarr (Isle of Wight). On the whole the tradition of hospitality seems to have been well maintained by the monks, and the fear was expressed at the time of the dissolution that a 'decay of hospitality' would ensue.

Alms

The care of the poor was another charitable duty which fell upon the religious orders. There was in the first place a general obligation incumbent upon all to distribute the 'broken meats' or 'left-overs' after meals to the local paupers who came to the abbey gates to receive this regular dole. Whether this routine was still regularly observed in the sixteenth century we have no direct evidence. We do know, however, from visitation records, that enquiries were from time to time made into the way in which this duty was performed, and that the visitors were not always satisfied with what they discovered. At St. Benet's Holme (Norfolk) in 1526 the poor were suffering because the dogs in the house, of which there was an excessive number, were consuming all the scraps and leaving nothing to be distributed. Six years later there were still too many dogs there for the visitor's liking, but the plight of the paupers was not mentioned. At West Acre the poor were also being deprived of their broken meats, though there was no suggestion there that dogs were to blame. At Markby (Lincs.), on the other hand, the poor were in 1519 enjoying the comfort of the canons' hall instead of being fed at the gates. This over-indulgence was thought to be as serious a fault as giving their food to the dogs.

Besides this daily distribution of broken meats, the monks and nuns at many houses were also obliged by the terms of the wills of various benefactors to distribute certain alms, generally in the form of food and drink, to a prescribed number of paupers at certain stated festivals, or in commemoration of certain anniversaries. About these prescribed charities we know a great deal in detail since their annual

c

cost was an allowable deduction when the monasteries, along with the rest of the church in England, were assessed for the new royal tax of the Tenth in 1535. In the *Valor Ecclesiasticus*, which is the record of that tax assessment, we can find them all set out. The proportion of the total income of the monasteries which was consumed by these obligatory charities was very small indeed. At Westminster, for example, out of a total gross revenue of more than £3,900 a year, only £104, or approximately 2·7%, was spent each year in this way. At Fountains the proportion was 1·7%, at St. Werburg's Chester, 1·3%, and at Syon (Middlesex) as little as 0·3%. There were, however, exceptions. At Whalley (Lancs.) as much as 22·1% of the abbey's income, that is to say £122 out of £551, was annually set aside to meet the cost of obligatory charities. £41 12*s.* of this sum went to maintain twenty-four paupers year in year out within the abbey itself. £62 8*s.* each year was spent on the weekly distribution of two quarters of grain. The remaining £18 went to provide special doles at Christmas and on Maundy Thursday. Great Malvern (Worcs.), with an annual income of £453, was committed to a wide list of charitable benefactions which consumed £50, or 11% of its total resources. At Norwich cathedral priory 8.4%, and at St. Peter's Gloucester 6·6% of income went on alms. These higher percentages, however, are too few in number to raise significantly the national average which stands at less than 2½%.

On the strength of this last figure some writers have claimed that monastic charity was a mere trifle, and that the lot of the poor cannot have been appreciably worsened by the dissolution of the monasteries. We must, however, remember that the commissioners who sent in the surveys upon which the *Valor Ecclesiasticus* is based were not required to take note of every charitable expense which the monks or nuns incurred, but only to set down those which the religious could show that they were legally obliged to undertake. If the commissioners in other parts of the country were as strict in the performance of their task as was Stephen Gardiner, bishop of Winchester, who explained that in surveying the property of the church in Hampshire he had 'extended to the uttermost' the value of every living, we can quite safely assume that the *Valor* gives us only a minimum figure for monastic charity. However freehanded the monks and nuns may have been in other ways, the tax assessors were not interested, and took no note. It was left to those other commissioners, who in the following years were charged with the task of dissolving the monasteries, to record here and there the presence of poor people who were entirely dependent upon the charity of the monks or nuns. Yet even the suppression commissioners take note of such people in an irregular and spasmodic manner. It was no part of their task to take a complete census of the recipients of monastic alms. They were, however, required to make a list of all the people actually living in each of the religious houses which came within their purview. When, therefore, they found, as at Stanley (Wilts.) seven almsmen, or, as at Garendon (Leics.) 'five impotent persons living there by alms', or, as at Broomholm (Norfolk) three persons 'found of alms', or, as at Nunkeeling (Yorks.) 'a poor woman found of charity' the presence of these persons in the appropriate cloister was duly noted. But where the charity of the monks did not extend to the offer of lodging there was no obligation upon the suppression commissioners to make any record either of the numbers who received regular alms or of the form that those alms took. Just occasionally a particularly hard case gets a mention in a marginal note

'*Memorandum* that there is an old poor and lame woman in the said house'

as though the commissioners were uncertain what action to take.

We must be careful, therefore, not to make sweeping statements about the amount or the effectiveness of monastic charity. We are largely ignorant of its true extent, and are likely to remain so. Even at the time of the dissolution contemporary opinion was itself divided on this point. On the one hand Simon Fish, the pamphleteer, claimed that even the obligatory alms were being neglected

'Divers of your noble predecessors, kings of this realm, have given lands to monasteries to give a certain sum of money yearly to poor people, whereof for the ancienty of the time they give never one penny'.

On the other hand, Robert Aske, the leader of the great rebellion known as the Pilgrimage of Grace, was equally clear that

'In the north parts much of the relief of the commons was by succour of abbeys'.

Corrodies and Annuities

Besides offering hospitality to the traveller and assistance to the poor, the religious orders also performed another, and probably less well-known, service to the community by the granting of annuities and corrodies. The distinction between the two, which is, however, not always consistently maintained even by contemporaries, is one of detail rather than of principle. An annuitant entered into an agreement with a religious house whereby, in return for a substantial cash payment, the monks undertook to pay him a fixed sum annually, generally for the remainder of his life. The monks thus had the benefit of the cash in hand, and the annuitant a secure income for the future. The amount of the annuity would naturally depend upon the size of the purchase payment and the expectation of life of the annuitant. Annuities of this type are, of course, available from most insurance companies today. A corrody was similar to an annuity, and sometimes the two terms are used interchangeably, but generally the corrodian received not cash but sustenance in kind in the form of food and shelter in or near the abbey. A corrodian, too, quite frequently purchased his corrody by a gift of livestock rather than by a cash payment. As a consequence of these differences in practice, annuitants and corrodians tended to come from rather different social backgrounds. The former were frequently men of means who sought a secure investment for some surplus capital. The latter were generally more humble folk who wanted security for their old age when the task of managing their own possessions was becoming too much for them.

Typical of this latter class of corrodians were Richard Loghan and his wife Agnes at the small Yorkshire nunnery of Handale. Their grant from the prioress and convent, which is set out in detail in the appendix to Chapter 6, entitled them to the use of a dwelling house, a daily ration of bread and ale, and regular supplies of meat, fish, grain, peat and wood for fires and candles for light. They were also, on feast days, to dine with the prioress and convent. What they had paid to secure all this is not recorded, but at another Yorkshire priory, Esholt, John and Agnes Hudson had purchased a similar, but not quite so generous, corrody by giving to the convent thirteen head of cattle, three calves, forty sheep, six wethers, thirty-four lambs and 20s. in cash. It was in 1518 that the Hudsons had secured the grant of their corrody. Between then and 1536 when the suppression commissioners took note of its details, John had died, but Agnes had continued to enjoy the benefits. She was by the latter date over 80 years of age, so that at the time that she and her husband had purchased the corrody she must have been 62 or more. At Yedingham Agnes Pykering and Richard Dobson had paid cash for similar corrodies, and Agnes Butterfield had offered certain cattle for another, but the deal had not been completed when the house was dissolved.

Not all annuities and corrodies were purchased. At some abbeys the heirs of the original benefactor retained the right to nominate a limited number of annuitants and were thus able to provide retirement pensions for faithful servants without putting themselves to any great expense. At some of the greater abbeys a considerable number of annuities of this kind were in the gift of the crown. In other cases annuities or corrodies were granted by the religious themselves to reward good service, to pension a retired abbot or prior, or even to provide wages in kind for some employee. An example of the last sort is provided by the case of Henry Wilkinson, chaplain to the nuns at Thicket (Yorks.). In place of the more usual purely cash stipend he was accustomed to receive the use of 'a chamber above the kitchen next the church', meat and drink 'as the prioress and convent have', the grazing of twenty sheep, the use of certain lands and of a little orchard which he had planted himself, and 46s. 8d. a year in cash.

Most annuities and corrodies were, however, the result of strictly business deals, and if the recipient lived longer than had been anticipated, or if the religious unwisely burdened themselves with too many payments of this kind, the financial results could be serious for them. From time to time the visitors had to step in, as at Bardney (Lincs.) in 1519 (see Appendix), and issue a warning against over-liberality in the grant of corrodies, or even prohibit their grant altogether. But, despite this episcopal oversight, there were, in 1536, some parts of the country where corrodians were rather too numerous for the comfort of their hosts. In the three counties of Leicester, Warwick and Rutland the suppression commissioners, during their tour of the smaller priories in that year, found no fewer than twenty-seven of these people distributed among eighteen houses which held a total of 155 monks and nuns. That is to say there was, on average, more than one corrodian to every six religious. This, however, seems to be an exceptionally high figure, and the other districts for which the suppression commissioners' reports are available show a much more modest proportion of corrodians to religious. In Hampshire, Wiltshire and Gloucestershire there were only thirteen corrodians in seventeen small houses containing 145 monks and nuns, but nine of them were concentrated in the seven Hampshire houses. In Yorkshire the corrodians were proportionately fewer still. At twelve small nunneries the commissioners found eight corrodians and 123 nuns. In Norfolk, at seventeen priories containing in all 75 monks and nuns there were only two corrodians, both at the same house. Taking the country as a whole, corrodies were probably not sufficiently numerous to be more than occasionally an embarrassment to some small priory which had unwisely granted too many.

The number of annuitants is not so easy to assess because of the difficulty created by the grant, in the years immediately preceding the suppression, of a large number of 'last minute' annuities. We know, for example, that one official of the Court of Augmentations, the government department set up in 1536 to supervise the dissolution of the monasteries, managed to persuade the monks and nuns of at least twenty-two houses to grant him annuities for life which together totalled £54 13s. 4d., nearly three times his official salary of £20. Although most of these annuities were granted within one year of the dissolution of the houses which made the grants, and were therefore subject to scrutiny and disallowance by the Court of Augmentations, they do not seem to have been challenged, and as late as 1555 the recipient was still in possession of an income of £47 6s. 8d. from this source.

At the Yorkshire Cistercian abbey of Kirkstall some fifty-one annuities were charged upon the revenues of the house after its dissolution. No individual annuity was very large, they ranged from 6s. 8d. to 60s. per annum in value, but in total they amounted to £58, that is to say to between one-fifth and one-sixth of the net annual value of the property of the suppressed abbey. Clearly the monks of Kirkstall would never in normal circumstances have burdened themselves with so great a number of annuities. They must have been fairly certain that dissolution was coming when they chose either to favour their friends with freely granted pensions which they knew they would not themselves have to pay, or else to obtain the maximum cash in hand by the widespread sale of annuities. The crown, their successor, was left burdened with all these payments without enjoying the benefit of the purchase money. Nor was Kirkstall exceptional. At Whitby, another Yorkshire house, there were forty-seven annuities totalling £101 19s., or nearly one-quarter of the net valuation. At

Meaux, in Holderness, there was a smaller, but still substantial number of annuities, twenty-one, amounting to £25 in total value, or about one-twelfth of the net valuation. At quite a number of other abbeys similar long lists of annuitants are to be found. Clearly we cannot accept these lavish grants as normal practice. And yet, as most of our information about monastic annuities comes from documents of the dissolution and post-dissolution years, it is very difficult to do more than guess what the normal practice in the making of such grants was.

It is evident, however, that the idea of annuities was not suddenly thought up at the dissolution, and that from time to time some of the larger abbeys did act as insurance offices in this way. It is not likely, on the other hand, that any house would in normal circumstances be so improvident as to burden itself with more than a handful of annuitants at any one time. For the layman who had a little money to spare a monastic annuity provided a safe investment. For the monks the sale of an annuity could be a convenient way of anticipating income, and might prove useful when they were faced with some unexpected or exceptional expenditure. We must not regard the annuitants as parasites, nor the monks who paid them as improvident. An annuity could bring advantages to both parties, and the financial facilities which the religious orders accorded to both annuitants and corrodians must be reckoned among the social services provided by the monks and nuns in the days before the dissolution.

APPENDIX: A BISHOP'S VISITATION

(From Visitations in the Diocese of Lincoln, 1517–1531, vol. II, pp. 77–8, Lincoln Record Society, vol. 35, 1944. Bardney, one of the more important Benedictine houses of the shire, lay about nine miles east of Lincoln city. The following extract is the account of bishop Atwater's visitation in 1519 which was recorded in his register after the event. It is a reasonably typical sample of this class of records. The bishop reproves the monks for keeping too many pets, for permitting their barber to give preference to secular customers, for slackness in singing mass and for the poor state of their service books, for breaking bounds and for granting corrodies too freely. Discipline at Bardney is clearly lax, but no major scandal is revealed. Latin is still the official language of the Church and of its records, though depositions of witnesses and quotations of words actually spoken in controversy are by this time usually recorded in English.)

BARDENAY MONASTERIUM

VISITACIO exercita ibidem in domo capitulari die Sabbati nono die Julii anno domini millesimo quingentesimo XIX^{no} per dominum Willelmum Atwater episcopum Lincolniensem personaliter.

Provideatur ne aliqui ex monachis monasterii custodiant aliquos canes venaticos infra loca claustralia monasterii, ne deturpetur per huiusmodi canes ecclesia, claustrum, refectorarium, domus capitularis. Dominus firmiter iniunxit omnibis monachis illius monasterii quod amodo nullus ipsorum aliquos canes venaticos aut nidos seu aves alias consimiles custodiet, habebit aut servabit in locis claustralibus monasterii seu in aliquibas aliis locis ullo modo.

Barbitonsor monachorum contra antiquum morem monasterii radit personas seculares in illa domo in qua radet monachos, et plerumque anteponit seculares huiusmodi in nocumentum confratrum monasterii. Dominus firmiter iniunxit quod amodo nullo pacto barbitonsor monachorum radet aliquas personas seculares in illa domo in qua sunt monachi monasterii radendi, neque quod ipse barbitonsor aliquas personas seculares anteponit monachos monasterii in huiusmodi rasuris, sed quod diligenciam debitam in rasura monachorum faciet.

Missa de beata virgine Marie non cantatur tanto numero monachorum ut deberet, nam pro maiori parte non sunt presentes ultra duo aut tres monachi, et tamen omnes deberent interesse scientes cantare. Eciam libri de missa beate virginis sunt lacerate fracte et obfuscate, incuria cantoris ad cuius officium spectat huiusmodi librorum reparacio et ligatura. Dominus iniunxit quod omnes monachi monasterii nedum scientes cantare sed eciam alii quicumque intererunt in missa beate virginis singulis diebus, exceptis tantummodo officiariis ad extra.

Fratres Robertus Bardenay et Ricardus Bardenay non surgunt ad matutinas. Non servant se in locis claustralibis sed plerumque illicenciati egrediuntur monasterium in villam de Bardenay, et eciam alias ceremonias et observancias sue religionis omittunt, et negligenter ac indevote agunt.

Dominus iniunxit omnibus monachis monasterii quod deinceps ipsi omnes abstinebunt a familiaritate secularium et quod servabunt se in locis claustralibus non egrediendo ullo pacto huiusmodi loca sine licencia, et quod non admittantur aliquas mulieres ad loca claustralia ullo pacto, sed cum omni diligencia divinis insistent.

Provideatur ne deinceps concedantur aliqua corrodia absque maturo tractatu et evidenti utilitate monasterii, et presertim eatenus quousque corrodia moderna extinguantur. Dominus strictius quo potuit iniunxit domino abbati quod ipse deinceps nullo modo concedat alicui aliqua corrodia et sic eciam omnibus monachis ibidem iniunxit.

Et deinde factis premissis iniunctionibus dominus ipsos in caritate cum Dei et sua benedictione dimisit et visitacionem suam ibidem dissolvit.

3

The Quality of Religious Life

IN the two preceding chapters we have been concerned mainly with the place of the religious orders in society, with their activities as landowners and with the social services which they provided. Now, to complete our picture of the English monasteries on the eve of their dissolution, we must look at the monks and nuns themselves and endeavour to determine how closely, in their daily lives, they adhered to the high ideals of the first founders of their orders.

Here we find ourselves at once on ground that was at one time highly controversial. On the one hand there were those to whom it was quite clear that the religious orders were irredeemably sunk in iniquity. The evidence in support of their view would seem at first sight to be overwhelming. First of all there is the bald, and oft-quoted assertion in the preamble to the act for the dissolution of the lesser monasteries (see appendix to Chapter 5) that

'manifest sin, vicious, carnal and abominable living'

is the daily practice among many of the religious. Then, to back up this statement in the statute, there are the reports of the royal visitors, who toured the monasteries in the autumn and winter of 1535–6, which reveal a truly deplorable state of depravity, and their many letters to their master, the King's vicar-general, Thomas Cromwell, which amplify their very terse reports with fulsome details in individual cases.

The Official View Criticised

But opposed to those who accepted all this evidence of iniquity at its face value were those who disregarded it all as so much government propaganda deliberately fabricated in order to blacken the good name of the religious orders and facilitate their suppression. Those who doubted the honesty and veracity of the royal visitors found comfort in contemporary and near-contemporary episcopal visitations which present a rather more favourable picture, and also pointed out some glaring inconsistencies in the government case. The iniquitous living described in the preamble to the suppression act is there attributed expressly only to the smaller religious houses which it is the purpose of the act to dissolve. The preamble then goes on to distinguish between these small and wicked priories and the

'divers and great solemn monasteries of this realm wherein, thanks be to God, religion is right well kept and observed'

implying thus that the dissolution of the lesser monasteries would be an act of reformation whereby the really corrupt and irredeemable houses would be swept away while their former inhabitants would be rehabilitated by being transferred to larger and more virtuous convents. But this distinction between great and honourable and small and wicked houses is not at all apparent in the reports of the king's visitors where, on the contrary, it is the larger abbeys which generally appear in the worse light. Thus the suppression act and the visitors' reports upon which it must be presumed to be based are quite inconsistent with each other.

Furthermore, the dissolution act is inconsistent in itself. Its preamble divides the great abbeys from the small on the basis of population, houses with twelve or more inhabitants being counted as large. In the operative clauses of the act, however, the division is made on the basis of income, houses with net annual revenues of £200 or more being exempt from suppression. These two systems of classification by no means produce the same result. There were many abbeys and priories with more than twelve inhabitants but less than £200 a year in income. These, according to the preamble, were 'great solemn monasteries', and yet the act declared them dissolved. On the other hand, some of the abbeys worth more than £200 a year had fewer than twelve inhabitants. They were spared by their wealth from immediate dissolution, despite their allegedly vicious and carnal living. Given these inconsistencies in the government case against the monasteries, it has been argued that there is good reason for mistrusting the veracity of official sources and for supposing that they present a deliberately falsified picture of the state of the religious orders.

A further good reason for being mistrustful of official sources, it is also often argued, lies in the speed with which we know that the royal visitation of the monasteries was carried out. The king's visitors began their work in the south and west in the late summer of 1535 and ended in the north in February 1536. The northern visitation was carried out by Richard Layton and Thomas Legh, and we know from their extant letters that they could not have begun that part of their work before 22 December 1535. On 28 February 1536 they claimed that they had finished. In the intervening period of just six days more than two months they reported upon the state of affairs at more than 120 religious houses scattered over a wide area. Their rate of progress works out at very nearly two visits a day, despite the great distances over bad roads in winter conditions which separated some of the remoter abbeys. Could Layton and Legh really have done all that they claimed to have done in the time available to them? Could any visitation so hastily conducted have produced anything but a distorted picture of the northern monasteries? So run the arguments of those who are not prepared to accept the testimony of the *Compendium Compertorum*, or 'Book of findings', which Layton and Legh produced after their northern tour.

The *Compendium Compertorum*

But before we dismiss the *Compendium Compertorum* as entirely worthless we must, in fairness to its compilers, look a little more closely at their method of working, and at the nature of their reports. In the first place it must be observed that Layton and Legh did not always travel in company and that each was perfectly capable of conducting a vigorous visitation on his own. It must also be pointed out that occasionally the visited attended upon the visitor instead of, as was the more usual practice, waiting for the visitor to come to their house. Thus, for example, the nuns of Esholt in Airedale went in a body to St. Oswald's near Pontefract to meet Dr. Legh, and so saved the visitor a journey of nearly twenty miles. In the third place we should remember that not every mention of a priory in the *Compendium* need necessarily mean that the visitors reached that house, or even had its inhabitants come to them.

A closer examination of this notorious document reveals that it is almost tabular in form. No more than five items of information are given under the heading of each monastery, and in the same order in every case. These items are: first, the names of those monks or nuns declared guilty of certain offences against the vow of chastity; secondly, the names of those who want to be released from their vows and to leave the cloister; thirdly, what the visitors call the 'superstition' of the house, that is to say the relic or relics held in especial esteem there; fourthly, the name of the 'founder' of the house, that is to say the living heir of the first benefactor who was regarded as having a hereditary and particular interest in the affairs of the convent; and lastly, in round figures, the income of the house, and, where applicable, its debts. These five items of information are virtually the only ones given, and apparently the only ones which interested the visitors. At only four of the more than 120 houses reported on by them is there any mention of any crime or misdemeanour other than sexual irregularities. This suggests very strongly that the visitors were working to a very limited brief. Their principal task was to gather material for a campaign designed to bring celibacy and relics into disrepute, and the religious orders with them. Discontent within the cloister was also to be noted. The catalogue of founders' names would be useful as their interests would have to be provided for if dissolution were to take place, and the brief statements of rents and debts would give a quick indication of the solvency of the houses visited.

The compilation of information under this limited number of headings would not have taken up nearly as much time as the conducting of a full visitation of the episcopal type where every aspect of the life of the community was subject to scrutiny. Indeed, certain items of information, such as the names of founders, or the nature of the relics venerated at particular abbeys, might well be such common knowledge that their discovery would not require a visit to the houses concerned. When, therefore, we find that in the case of no fewer than thirty-four of the priories reported upon in the *Compendium Compertorum* the visitors have noted no more than rents, founders and sometimes relics, we have good grounds for suspecting that they may have passed these convents by. On the other hand, where sexual offences are noted the names of the offenders are invariably given, and we know that these names are not fictitious as so many of them can be confirmed from other sources. Such offenders, except perhaps in a few very notorious cases, are unlikely to have been known by name very far outside the walls of their own convents, so that where Layton and Legh take note of them we can be fairly sure that the house in question was actually visited.

And so, if we accept that Layton and Legh sometimes worked separately, that they did not necessarily visit every house that they reported on, and that where they did visit the scope of their enquiries was limited, we shall have reduced their northern visitation to manageable physical proportions. But are we bound, as a consequence, to accept as true the scandalous picture of monastic life which they present? We should first compare their findings with those of two other sets of contemporary reporters, the bishops' visitors and the suppression commissioners.

Bishops' Visitations

Of the records of episcopal visitations the most readily available are those from the dioceses of Lincoln and Norwich, already mentioned in Chapter 2 (p. 18). To these can be added a few from Worcester, Bath and Wells, York and elsewhere, but the number of cases in which we have the records of both episcopal and royal visitations of one and the same house within a period of time sufficiently short to make a comparison of value remains disappointingly small. One of the best examples is provided by the great Benedictine abbey of St. Mary's at York.

The archiepiscopal visitation of St. Mary's took place on 17 September 1534. The royal visitors, Layton and Legh, arrived to conduct their enquiries on 13 January 1536, a little less than sixteen months later. In anticipation of their visit they had written to Cromwell

'we suppose to find much evil disposition both in the abbot and the convent'

and they were not, apparently, disappointed in their hopes, for they were able to report that no fewer than seven of the brethren were practising homosexuals. Their expectations of the abbot were not, however, fulfilled. He does not appear among the accused. This is rather odd, because the abbot had been the only one to be singled out for mention by name by the archbishop's visitors little more than a year before. He was then accused of keeping suspiciously intimate company with a married woman and was ordered to abstain from associating with her in future. It would seem clear enough from this that there had been at the very least dubious rumours circulating about the abbot, and yet, if there had so recently been a scandal (the archbishop's injunctions in which he deals with the alleged affair were delivered to the abbey in August 1535, only five months before the arrival of the royal visitors) how did it escape the normally keen ears of Layton and Legh?

The answer is probably to be found in the circumstances attending the archbishop's visitation. The abbot had at first denied his right to visit, claiming exemption from episcopal oversight for his house. Finding, however, that his papal bulls of exemption were no longer treated with the same respect as formerly, he had been obliged to admit the archbishop's representatives. But then, before the visitation had been concluded by the presentation of the injunctions, the abbot had had the happy idea of appealing for protection to the new supreme ecclesiastical authority, Thomas Cromwell the king's vicar-general. Cromwell had taken the abbot's side, informed the archbishop that he had no authority over St. Mary's, and ordered him, somewhat abruptly, to abandon his visitation. The archbishop, however, seems to have decided that, whatever Cromwell might say, he would at least deliver his injunctions as some record of the lengthy proceedings which had by then been dragging on for nearly a year, and into these injunctions some measure of his personal pique against the abbot has perhaps been allowed to enter. The affair of the married woman receives undue prominence, and yet the archbishop finds nothing proved against the abbot. He enjoins no penance, but merely warns him that his conduct has been laying him open to grave suspicion. He is prepared to believe the worst about this troublesome abbot, but can do no better than repeat rumours.

On the other hand the royal visitors had no personal quarrel with the abbot. Indeed, as he was one of those who sat in parliament, whose goodwill would shortly be required to assist the passage of the act to dissolve the lesser monasteries, they may well have deemed it politic to overlook his minor aberrations.

Royal and Episcopal Visitations Compared

We can thus suggest plausible reasons why the episcopal and royal visitors should differ in their findings about the abbot of St. Mary's, but we are still left with a very substantial difference between their reports on the conduct of the other monks of the house. The archbishop's injunctions mention no member of the community other than the abbot by name, and the monks in general are criticised only for such minor matters as the wearing of fine clothing and the keeping of a wine shop in the precinct. There is not the smallest hint of such immorality as the king's visitors claim to have discovered so shortly afterwards. Are we then to conclude that the seven sinners named in the *Compendium* were blameless at the time of the archbishop's visitation, and that the community at St. Mary's underwent a sweeping moral degeneration in the sixteen months between the two visitations? Or are we to assume that the archbishop's representatives were either unwilling or unable to discover such sins which only the more searching investigations of Layton and Legh were able to unearth? Or must we reject the evidence of the *Compendium* as pure fabrication?

That the archbishop's visitors were capable of discovering immorality, and that Layton and Legh did not always invent evil for the sake of denigrating the religious, is readily apparent from the case of another Yorkshire house, the small Cistercian nunnery of Esholt, where once again the findings of the two sets of visitors can be directly compared. This priory received the archbishop's vicar-general, Dr. Clyff, some time before 10 September 1535. Legh interrogated the nuns at St. Oswald's some time in January or February 1536. The archbishop's injunctions contain a great deal that was almost common form after such visitations; exhortations and prohibitions relating to obedience to the prioress, locking the doors at night, not admitting strangers to the dorter, keeping silence in the choir and cloister, and so on. But there are among these general-purpose injunctions two of specific application to Esholt alone. In the first place it is noted that the nunnery was not well enough walled about, especially on the south side of the cloister where a public way ran down to a bridge over the river Aire. In the second place it is reported that one of the nuns, Joan Hutton by name

'hath lived incontinently and unchaste and hath brought forth a child of her body begotten'.

For this serious lapse, which the visitor stigmatises as a 'horrible crime', the offending nun was

'to remain in prison or in some secret chamber within the dorter'.

1 Durham Cathedral: view from the south, showing the cloister and the other surviving monastic buildings

2 Mount Grace: a Carthusian priory in Yorkshire. This view from the south-west clearly shows the distinctive features of the Carthusian plan: the modest size of the church and the individual cells and gardens arranged round the great cloister

No one was to speak to her without licence of the prioress, she was to fast on Wednesday and Fridays, and her punishment was to continue for two years, unless the archbishop should otherwise provide.

Presumably then sister Joan was still undergoing her punishment when the nuns of Esholt went to meet Dr. Legh, and, whether they took her with them or not, her sins could hardly have been concealed from the king's visitor. And so, as might be expected, her name and offence were duly recorded in the *Compendium*. But that is the limit of the agreement between the findings of the two visitations. For Dr. Clyff Joan Hutton was the only offender. Dr. Legh claims that another nun, Agnes Bayne, was guilty of the same offence as Joan, and that a third, Agnes Wood, though she had not become a mother, had behaved in every way as badly as her two sisters. Had Dr. Clyff not probed deeply enough into the affairs of the nunnery? Had the two Agnes's only fallen into sin in the four months separating the two visitations? Or was Dr. Legh indulging in a little fabrication?

In the six other Yorkshire cases in which this direct comparison between episcopal and royal visitations can be made the results are similar. The bishop finds no serious fault, but Layton and Legh find grievous sinners at every house.

In the diocese of Norwich, where the bishop, Richard Nix, made his last pre-dissolution visitation of the monasteries in 1532, three years before the royal visitors began their work, the result of a comparison between his findings and those of the latter is very similar to that obtained in Yorkshire. The rather longer interval between the two visitations which tends to make the Norwich comparisons less valuable, is to a certain extent counterbalanced by the fact that a greater number of individual comparisons, eighteen in all, can be made. At only one house, Coxford, is there any correspondence between the results of the two visitations. Here the bishop's visitor reported that one of the canons had fathered a child, but that he had been punished for his fault. The royal visitors also took note of one delinquent at this house. At ten of the other houses the bishop had various faults to find; slackness and quarrels, maladministration and unauthorised comforts, but nowhere any of the serious sexual irregularities which the royal visitors claimed to have found at every house but one. At the remaining seven convents the bishop declared that all was well, but the royal visitors named no fewer than twenty-one offenders.

D

Comparisons of this sort can be repeated in other parts of the country with very similar results. Generally speaking the bishops' visitations do show that grave moral lapses of the kind with which the *Compendium* is filled did from time to time occur, as at Greenfield (Lincs.) in 1525 where one nun had given birth to a child, or at Littlemore (Oxfordshire) in 1517 where the prioress and one of the sisters were accused of the same offence.[1] But the incidence of such cases is spasmodic. They are exceptional rather than common, and nowhere near as frequent as the authors of the *Compendium* would have us believe. If we believe that the episcopal visitors by and large did their job fairly well then we must reject the *Compendium* as being largely the product of Layton and Legh's vivid imagination. If, on the other hand, we think that it was not very difficult for an errant community to hide its sins from the bishop's deputy on his not very frequent visits then we may be prepared to believe that the long list of offenders named in the *Compendium* is a tribute to the efficiency rather than the mendacity of the royal visitors.

Suppression Commissioners' Reports

Episcopal visitation records, however, provide the material for only one of the two tests we can apply to the *Compendium*. We can also compare the royal visitors' findings with the opinions of the commissioners appointed after the passage of the dissolution act of 1536 to carry out its provisions. These commissioners were not all government men, though the officials of the newly established court of Augmentations served with them and did most of the work. The first task that the suppression commissioners had to perform was to visit each religious house in their area which was small enough to be in danger of dissolution under the act, to compile complete inventories of all its possessions, and a list of all the people who had their living in it. They were also required to take note of the personal reputation of the religious, and this they duly did. The commissioners' comments survive for quite a wide variety of areas; Norfolk; Surrey and Sussex; Hampshire, Wiltshire and Gloucestershire; Leicestershire, Warwickshire and Rutland; and for parts of Lancashire and Yorkshire. Save for two cases in Surrey, two in Sussex, one in Warwickshire, four in Norfolk and three in Yorkshire, the verdict of the suppressors is

---

[1] See also the case of Elizabeth Lutton of Yedingham in the appendix to this chapter.

generally favourable, but only in Norfolk, Leicestershire and York-shire can direct comparisons be made between these commissioners' reports and the findings of the royal visitors. In other areas not covered by the royal visitors' actual reports, the suppression com-missioners' returns can sometimes, but not very frequently, be com-pared with descriptions given by the royal visitors in their letters to Cromwell.

In Leicestershire only three houses figure both in the *Compendium* and in the suppression commissioners' returns, and of these Layton and Legh had evil to report of two. The commissioners, however, ex-pressed their entire satisfaction with the 'good and virtuous conversa-tion' of the inhabitants of all three. The conflict of evidence could hardly be more direct.

In Yorkshire, where the commissioners' and visitors' reports upon eleven small priories may be compared, there is a significantly greater measure of agreement between the two. At eight of the eleven houses the suppression commissioners had no fault to find. At four of these eight the royal visitors were equally unable to find any evil. At a fifth Layton and Legh reported that one nun would like to be released from her vows, but the commissioners found her still in the cloister, and anxious to remain. Otherwise the two reports agreed that all was well. At a sixth house, Baysdale, the royal visitors accused the ex-prioress, Joan Fletcher, of a serious lapse. The suppression com-missioners did not include her name in their list of the nuns there, and were able to give the priory a good report. Thus in as many as six out of eight cases there is no serious discrepancy between the findings of the commissioners and those of the visitors.

At each of the houses to which they could not give good reports the Yorkshire commissioners made marginal notes opposite the name of one nun to indicate that she was guilty of some serious but unspecified offence. At Swine the name so marked was that of Elizabeth Copelay, whom Layton and Legh had also singled out for special mention. Here, then, is just one more case where the commissioners' reports and the *Compendium* are not in conflict. At Kirklees the com-missioners took note of the sins of Isabel Rhodes, but the visitors attributed her fault to Joan Kyppax. Perhaps here Layton or Legh jotted down the wrong name in his haste. But even if we accept this explanation and thus bring the total number of Yorkshire cases in which our two sources are virtually agreed up to eight, we are still left with three instances where the divergence between them is too great to be easily explained away. At Esholt the commissioners duly noted the name of Joan Hutton, who was presumably still undergoing the punishment prescribed by the archbishop. They did not, however, find any fault with the two Agnes's whom, as we saw above (p. 37) Dr. Legh had added to the list of sinners at that house. At Handale the royal visitors reported that Alice Brampton had become a mother. Four months later the suppression commissioners declared firmly that the nuns at this house were 'all of good living' and recorded Alice's age as 70. At Yedingham, so the visitors said, Agnes Butterfield had sinned in similar fashion. Once again the commissioners reported that all there were 'of good name and living' and gave Agnes' age as 49.

In Wiltshire the commissioners reported that all at Maiden Bradley were 'of honest conversation' where only a few months previously Dr. Layton had waxed humorous at the expense of the prior and his six children, tall sons and marriageable daughters. In Norfolk the commissioners' reports cover sixteen houses of which thirteen had a few months earlier been reported on by the royal visitors who found some evil to record of all save the nuns of Carrow in Norwich. The suppression commissioners agreed that these last were 'of very good name'. They were also in general agreement with the visitors about the canons of Thetford where they found one 'of slender report', the nuns of Mareham where there were five 'of slanderous report', and the canons at Wendling whose name, they said, was 'not good'. But this measure of agreement between commissioners and visitors is more than cancelled out by their complete disagreement in the nine other cases in Norfolk where such comparisons can be made. To the commissioners the religious at all these nine were 'of good' or 'of very good name' despite the fact that so short a time before the visitors had found one or more sinners in every cloister.

The general result of comparing the royal visitors' reports with the comments of the suppression commissioners is thus similar to that obtained by comparing the former with the bishops' visitations. We must believe either that the commissioners were not so thorough in their investigations or else that Layton and Legh and the other royal visitors were ready to take suspicion for proof and to add imaginary to real offences. In only a very few instances can all three types of report be compared together, and where this is

NEW FEBRUARY PENGUINS

(Fiction and non-Fiction)

Modern Classics

John Hersey
Hiroshima (Reissue) 30p
Henry James
The Awkward Age (Reissue) 45p
Jack Kerouac
On the Road 40p
Thomas Mann
Little Herr Friedemann and Other Stories 35p
Virginia Woolf
Between the Acts (Reissue) 30p

Fiction

Saul Bellow
Mr Sammler's Planet 30p
Richard Condon
Mile High 40p
The Oldest Confession 35p
Bernard Malamud
Pictures of Fidelman 25p
L. Woiwode
What I'm Going to Do, I Think 35p
Penguin Modern Stories 10
Brian Glanville, Janice Elliott,
Jennifer Dawson, Paul Winstanley,
Jean Stubbs 30p

Non-Fiction

Alfred Douglas
The Oracle of Change 35p
Ogden Nash
There's Always Another Windmill 30p

All these books can be obtained
from your bookseller or, in case of
difficulty, from J. Barnicoat
(Falmouth) Ltd, P.O. Box 11,
Falmouth, Cornwall. When
ordering by post please enclose
cost of books plus 5p per volume
postage and packing.

THE PENGUIN
MEDICAL ENCYCLOPEDIA

PETER WINGATE

Hippocrates asserted, over two
thousand years ago, that a
doctor must teach his patients
to care for their own health.
Until recently, however, most
doctors have preferred to believe
that patients can know too
much.

This encyclopedia is addressed
to anyone who is concerned with
the care of sick people in
particular to the patient himself,
who should be the doctor's
principal colleague. At the same
time Dr Wingate (who regularly
broadcasts on medical topics) is
emphatic that it is not a 'Home
Doctor' or do-it-yourself
medical manual.

In hundreds of entries, running
from *abdomen* to *zymosis,* he
deals with the body and mind in
health and sickness, with drugs
and surgery, with the history,
institutions and vocabulary of
the profession and with many
other aspects of medical science.
In the course of these Dr
Wingate clearly explains the
principles involved in the
diagnosis and treatment of a
thousand and one illnesses from
the inconvenience of baldness
to the rigours of cancer. 60p

done, as at Esholt, the result is generally to the discredit of the royal visitors.

The General Picture

Nevertheless the general picture of sixteenth-century monasticism which emerges from the contemporary record is not a very happy one. For the testimony of the king's visitors to have been at all credible to their contemporaries, the religious must have had no very outstanding reputation for virtue to begin with. Had the religious houses been filled one and all with spirited devotees of the monastic life, had the general reputation of the monks and nuns been good, the exaggerated calumnies of Layton and Legh and their fellow visitors would never have obtained such wide credit. The government case against the monasteries could never have been based so firmly on the moral issue had the general slackness and lack of enthusiasm among the orders not bred in the lay public a widespread lack of sympathy with the religious ideal, and predisposed them to believe the worst.

For monks and nuns to justify their existence in the eyes of an increasingly secular world it was not enough that they should live lives of moderate piety and engage in good works. Laymen could do as well; monks must do better. They must be seen to possess superior spiritual gifts and to live lives above reproach. For the most part the monks and nuns of England and Wales on the eve of the dissolution fell short of this requirement. Yet they were not, on the other hand, negligent of their duties. They still recited the offices, opened their doors to travellers, cared in their own fashion for the poor and the aged, and served the community in many other ways. But all that they did could equally well have been done by others. Even in the celebration of intercessory masses they had no monopoly. Since the fourteenth century an increasing number of chantry priests had been fulfilling the same function, and it was not easy to argue that the prayers of a convent had any greater efficacy than those of a single priest. On every count the religious were expendable. And yet that inertia which is such a potent force in any society kept the monasteries going. Recruits still came in. They may not all have been volunteers, but they sufficed to keep the orders going. Most of the abbeys and priories had nearly 400 years of corporate life behind them, and some had stood for very much longer. They were part of the accepted order of society. But when some men began to have doubts about the efficacy of propitiatory masses and others began to cast envious eyes upon the lands and possessions of the orders, when people began to ask what purpose they served, then the religious communities were unlikely to be allowed for long to survive unless they could claim to do something that no other person or organisation could do as well. With the important exception of the Carthusians (who were recruiting new members so fast that there was a waiting list for admission to the new cells being built at Mount Grace in Yorkshire), the Observant Franciscans and the Bridgettines, the religious orders were unable to meet this challenge. Indeed a remarkable number of them were only too willing, when the crisis came, to accept without protest the sudden extinction of their time-honoured way of life.

APPENDIX:

THE HAZARDS OF LIFE IN THE CLOISTER

(Two closely associated factors which must have contributed significantly to the occurrence of apostasy and violation of their vows among nuns were the early age at which many of them were professed, and the fact that some entered the cloister against their will. Both these points are well illustrated by the following narrative of the adventures of Elizabeth Lutton of Yedingham which is based closely on the records of Star Chamber and the Archbishop's court at York.)

THE STORY OF ELIZABETH LUTTON

ELIZABETH LUTTON was the daughter of Stephen Lutton, eldest son and heir apparent of William Lutton of Knapton. About the year 1512, when she was fourteen years of age, she

'entered into religion and was veiled in the habit of a nun of the order of St. Benedict in the priory of Yedingham'

which was only a few miles from her home. She underwent there a year's probation before she took her vows. According to the testimony of her fellow nuns she made her profession willingly and showed no signs of distress on that solemn occasion, but subsequently she was heard to say, more than once,

'that she was professed nun against her will'

And yet, said the other nuns,

'she never spake it openly before the prioress of the house nor never made open reclamation nor protestation of her dissent' but only complained

'after the way and manner of light communication as well with seculars as with religious'

for she was

'much given to communication and talking'.

Yet all went well for more than ten years, until 1525, the last year in office of prioress Elizabeth Whitehead, when Elizabeth Lutton was found to have conceived a child and was, for this reason, cut off from all association with the other nuns and placed in a house out-side the cloister, but within the precinct of the nunnery. There she remained until her child was born. It was probably during this period that Sir Robert Constable encountered her as he came

'riding from his place of Flamborough to Sir Roger Cholmeley's house his son-in-law'.

The latter lived at Thornton-in-Pickering-Lythe, and as his route thence from Flamborough lay close to Yedingham, Sir Robert

'called at the said nunnery which is nigh the highway to the intent to drink with the prioress'.

The prioress was away, but two of the nuns greeted the traveller and prevailed upon him to take a 'cup of ale'. Afterwards, when he and the nuns were in the priory church, he saw Elizabeth Lutton

'looking out at a window on high looking into the church'

so that, although segregated from her sisters, she was not cut off altogether from the services of the church. Sir Robert's interest was aroused, and he insisted upon meeting and cross-questioning the offending nun. From her he quickly learned, according to his own account, both that she was pregnant and that

'she was brought to religion and professed against her will as part of her sisters knew right well'.

After the birth of her child Elizabeth, aided by the intercessions of the nuns' confessor, was readmitted to the cloister by the new prioress, Agnes Braydericke. Her sins were forgiven her (the fate of the baby is not mentioned anywhere in the record) and she lived and behaved herself as a nun once more until about the year 1532 when she became involved in a train of events which resulted in her leaving the convent rather abruptly. Since Elizabeth had entered the nunnery her father, Stephen Lutton, had died without other issue, leaving her as his sole heir. Her grandfather, William Lutton, had, however, on the occasion of the marriage of his second and surviving son Thomas (Elizabeth's uncle), been persuaded to regard Elizabeth as dead to the world and to re-settle all his property upon Thomas and his heirs. In due course William had died and Thomas had entered into the family inheritance. But in 1531 or 1532 this same Thomas Lutton, who was for some of his lands a tenant of the powerful Sir Robert Constable, had dared to participate in an inquest verdict damaging to the interests of the latter, who at once threatened revenge and seems to have remembered his encounter with Elizabeth at Yedingham, for shortly afterwards (though Sir Robert, of course, denied that he had had any part in the affair) a certain Thomas Scaseby descended upon the nunnery accompanied by a group of Sir Robert's servants, and

> 'Laboured and procured the said Elizabeth Lutton, being a nun professed, to depart out of the said nunnery and to forsake her religion, and thereupon conveyed her out of the said house'.

The chief purpose behind this abduction was to revive Elizabeth's claim to the Lutton inheritance, to the great discomfort of her uncle Thomas who had thought her safely out of the way. An incidental result of the raid was Elizabeth's marriage to Thomas Scaseby, who may well have been the man responsible for her earlier lapse. The success or failure of Elizabeth's claim to the family lands, and the issue of the case between her uncle and Sir Robert are not on record, but she does not appear to have returned to Yedingham.

Throughout the story Elizabeth appears as one to whom life in the cloister made no particular appeal. Though afraid to complain openly to the prioress she had lost no opportunity of making her discontent known to others. At the time of her profession she was probably not sole heir to her father as in that case he would have had little difficulty in finding her a husband and no particular reason for wanting to place her in a nunnery against her will. And yet her father, at the time of his death, had no other issue, so that any brothers or sisters she may have had must have died before their father, leaving Elizabeth as sole surviving heir, and a person of much greater consequence than at the time of her profession, and one well suited to Sir Robert Constable's schemes for revenge. Thomas Scaseby undoubtedly used the strength of Elizabeth's claim to her grandfather's estates as an inducement to her to leave the cloister, but it is doubtful if much persuasion was necessary. Even allowing for the early attainment of maturity in her generation, fourteen was a very early age for any girl to be required to abjure the world for the rest of her life. It is not to be wondered at that one who took the veil so young first fell a victim to the seducer, and then, having undergone strict punishment for her sin, was ready to fly from the cloister in the hope of an inheritance which would make her independent. Nor was Elizabeth's early profession exceptional. From the testimony of her nine sister nuns we learn that one was professed at twelve years of age, two at thirteen, two at fourteen, one at fifteen, one at sixteen, one at twenty, and the prioress at twenty-one or twenty-two.

Section II

The Dissolution

4

The Preliminaries

THE fate which befell the English religious orders in the 1530s was not without precedent. The confiscation of the endowments of monastic houses in order to convert them to other uses was not in itself a revolutionary idea. Almost a century before the accession of Henry VIII, when Henry V had led England into war with France, the alien priories (small religious houses in England dependent upon mother houses in France) had been obliged to sever their foreign connections or suffer expropriation. At about the same time, as we have seen (p. 4 above), a much more sweeping secularisation of church property had been proposed in parliament.

Precedents for Dissolution

From time to time, both before and after the dissolution of the alien priories, it had also been thought advisable to terminate the life of individual small convents which had fallen on hard times either because their revenues were no longer sufficient to support an active community or because new recruits were not coming forward and the few survivors were unable to maintain the religious life in the proper manner. Such occasional suppressions were usually undertaken on the initiative of a bishop or other prominent churchman, and normally required papal licence. A good example is provided by the suppression in 1497, by John Alcock, bishop of Ely, of St. Radegund's nunnery in Cambridge, and the conversion of its buildings and revenues to the foundation of Jesus college there. John Fisher, bishop of Rochester, and founder of St. John's college in the same university, also secured the suppression of two nunneries to help its endowment.

These were, of course, limited exercises in suppression which had little impact upon the monastic world in general. A rather more extensive operation was undertaken by Wolsey in the 1520s when, in imitation of Alcock and Fisher, he set about the foundation not only of a college at Oxford but also of a grammar school in his native Ipswich. To finance these new foundations he secured papal permission for the suppression of twenty-nine assorted religious houses which ranged in size from St. Frideswide's in Oxford which housed fifteen canons and was worth more than £200 a year to the humble priory of Tiptree in Essex which had only two canons and £22 a year to its name. It is very significant for the history of the later royal suppressions that Wolsey's chief agent in carrying out this work was none other than Thomas Cromwell, then just beginning to make a reputation for himself as an able administrator in the service of the cardinal.

To these native precedents for the suppression of religious houses can be added some important foreign examples, notably that of Gustavus Vasa, the usurping, dynasty-founding king of Sweden. By his Västerås Recess of 1527 he secured the conversion of a substantial proportion of Swedish church property, including that of the monasteries, to the support of his government and the enrichment of his followers among the nobility. Some of the Lutheran princes of Germany has also profited from the anti-monastic elements in their new faith and confiscated the endowments of religious houses in their areas. The protestant cantons of Switzerland had done much the same. Thus there was clearly nothing sacrosanct about the property of the abbeys, and it was not unreasonable for an English king who was faced with ever-rising costs and yet had to put his country in a state of defence against the possibility of a papally-inspired crusade against him, to find salvation in the conversion of monastic possessions to the use of his government. The long passage in the preamble to the First Fruits and Tenths act of 1534 (26 Henry VIII c. 3) which recounts the benefits which Henry VIII has conferred on his people and speaks of the vast sums which he has expended in securing those benefits is not all artful propaganda. There is a considerable element of truth in the statement that the king

'daily sustaineth for the maintenance tuition and defence of this his realm and his loving subjects of the same . . . great excessive and inestimable charges'.

The Motive: Finance

Finance is indeed the key to the proper understanding of the dissolution. The official case against the monasteries rested on moral grounds, and the validity of that case has already been examined in the previous chapter, but the primacy of the financial consideration in governmental thinking is made plain by the adoption of a purely monetary line of distinction between the smaller abbeys with less than £200 net annual income which the dissolution act declared suppressed, and the larger abbeys which were to be allowed to survive. It is also to be seen in the title of the new government department established to supervise the dissolution and to administer the proceeds, the 'Court of the Augmentations of the Revenues of the King's Crown'. Nevertheless it is sometimes suggested, or at least implied, that other objectives were also in the minds of those who planned the great confiscation. Some have sought to link it more clearly with the rejection of the Roman jurisdiction caused by the king's matrimonial difficulties and his assumption of the headship of the church in England. It has been argued that the religious orders formed a reservoir of pro-papal sentiment in England which might endanger the security of the new royal régime if any serious attempt was made to overthrow it by a papally-inspired coalition of continental powers. What lends a little colour to this view is the fact that Henry VIII was first seriously threatened with excommunication in 1535, immediately before the first overt moves were made against the monasteries. It also seems significant that a high proportion of those who suffered execution for refusing to accept Henry's ecclesiastical supremacy were monks and friars.

A closer examination of the course of events, however, presents a rather different picture. It was in the spring of 1534, with the passage of the Succession act (25 Henry VIII c. 22) that every adult Englishman was first made liable to be required to take an oath accepting the validity of the king's second marriage and, by implication, rejecting the authority of the pope, who had given his judgment against it. Later in the same year the wording of the succession oath was altered to make the rejection of papal jurisdiction rather more explicit, and the Treasons act (26 Henry VIII c. 13) brought within danger of execution all who refused to take the revised oath. In the same year royal commissioners went to work throughout the kingdom proffering the oath to selected people and duly recording their acceptance of it. Every monk and friar was eventually required to swear, and the only ones who found any conscientious difficulty in so doing were a mere handful belonging chiefly to the Carthusian and Reformed Franciscan orders, two orders which had only a few houses each in England but were renowned for the rigour of their observance. The great majority of the English religious showed themselves ready enough to accept the new order. And why not? They were practically all Englishmen and shared the prejudice of their contemporaries against foreigners, a prejudice which had very materially assisted the king in his rejection of the authority of the bishop of Rome. Thus, before any steps had been taken towards dissolution, the loyalty of the religious had been put to the test and found satisfactory. The very small minority who refused the oath were dealt with in 1535, along with Sir Thomas More and John Fisher, and there was nothing in the demeanour of the surviving majority to suggest that they were politically dangerous.

Even if the monastic orders had formed a potentially disloyal group, would dissolution have been the right way to deal with them? Would dispersal from their cloisters and the forfeiture of their property have inclined papally-disposed monks to be any more loyal to the régime which dispossessed them? In fact one of the consequences of the dissolution act was to drive some of the dispossessed religious into association with the northern rebels in the Pilgrimage of Grace, while those whose abbeys had not yet been touched strove earnestly to avoid involvement. Dissolution was more likely to create than to remove opposition to the royal headship.

The Motive: Relics and Pilgrimages

There is, however, yet another aspect of the dissolution which is often overlooked and does suggest that the financial, though probably the chief motive, might not have been the only one at work. We have already observed how the monastic visitors of 1535–6 seem to have concentrated their attention almost exclusively upon sexual irregularities and the retention and veneration of relics of the saints. These visitors were of course acting upon instructions from Thomas Cromwell, the recently appointed vicar-general in ecclesiastical matters of the newly proclaimed royal head of the church. It is interesting then to observe further that Cromwell's two sets of general injunctions,

issued to the clergy in 1536 and 1538, also contain quite a determined attack upon the veneration of relics and the making of pilgrimages to the more famous shrines such as that of St. Thomas at
Canterbury or that of Our Lady at Walsingham. Most, though not
all, of these objects of pilgrimage were in the guardianship of the
religious orders. There is therefore a clear link between the dissolution of the monasteries and the campaign of the visitors and injunctions against relics and pilgrimages. Most commentators have been
inclined to regard the latter as subordinate to the former, and to
suggest that it was in order to discredit the religious orders still
further in popular estimation, and to facilitate their suppression, that
their long-treasured holy relics were first held up to ridicule and then
seized and destroyed by the government.

Of course the financial motive also comes in here, for some of the
more famous shrines were richly ornamented with gold and silver and
precious stones, and so could make substantial additions to the royal
stock of treasure. But it is also open to suggest that the attack upon
pilgrimages and relics had recommended itself to Cromwell on its
own merits, and that its independent origins have been obscured for
us by its coincidence in time with the dissolution of the monasteries.
Recent reconsiderations of Cromwell's character and career have
been rather more sympathetic than his earlier biographies, and have
seen in him something better than the ruthlessly efficient, personally
ambitious and irreligious administrator. Notice has been taken of his
patronage of churchmen of reformist views, of his part in securing
official approval for an English version of the Bible, and of his
anxiety to come to a political and theological understanding with
the German Lutherans. An aversion from the cult of images and
relics would be very much in keeping with such views and attitudes.
Furthermore, the campaign against relics and pilgrimages began in
1535, at a time when it is fairly clear that no more than a partial
dissolution, involving only the smaller abbeys, was intended. Yet it
was the larger houses which were more seriously affected by the
attack on shrines which reached its climax in 1538.

It is, of course, true that in many cases the pulling down of a
particular shrine was accompanied by the surrender of the abbey
which contained it. At Walsingham, for example, the image of Our
Lady was taken away on 14 July 1538 and the priory dissolved on
4 August. At Boxley the monks were dispersed on 29 January, and

The *Valor Ecclesiasticus*, 1535: part of the survey of the Augustinian priory of Maxstoke in Warwickshire, given in full in the appendix to Chapter 4

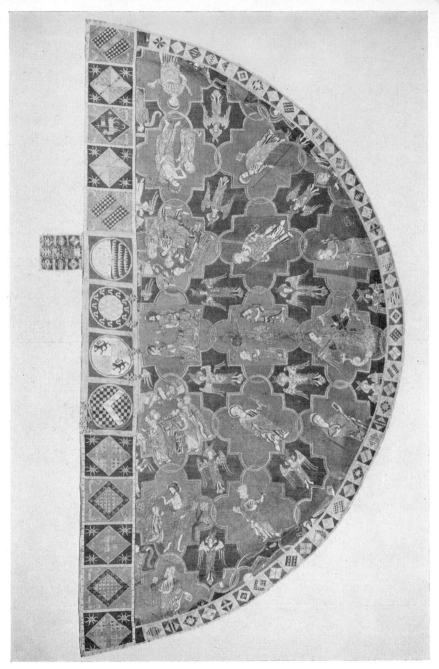

4 The Syon Cope: one of the best surviving examples of late medieval English needlework, and typical of the ornate vestments possessed by many of the monasteries. Made in the fourteenth century it belonged at the dissolution to the nuns of Syon in Middlesex who went into exile as a group, taking it with them. It is now in the Victoria and Albert Museum the workings of the famous mechanical rood were exposed to the London crowd on 24 February. But at Hailes, in contrast, nearly fourteen months elapsed between the seizure of the relic of the Holy Blood on 28 October 1538 and the surrender of the abbey on 24 December 1539. Similarly, at Winchester and Canterbury, where the shrines of St. Swithin and St. Thomas were destroyed in September 1538, the cathedral churches remained in the hands of the monks for more than a year longer. Winchester surrendered to the crown in November 1539, Canterbury in April 1540. In cases such as these the two operations, suppressing the shrine and evicting the monks, were clearly separate, and the second did not necessarily follow from the first. It is therefore open to us to suggest that the campaign for the destruction of relics and the putting down of pilgrimages was embarked upon initially on its own merits, and that only as the dissolution of the monasteries proceeded did the two operations tend to become linked. Indeed it may well be that Cromwell's desire to suppress relics and pilgrimages gave him another motive besides the financial one for turning against the religious orders in the first place.

And yet the financial aspect of the dissolution remains undoubtedly the most prominent. The standing resources of the crown were no longer adequate to meet the ever-increasing cost of government and defence, particularly the cost of ships and guns which were so important a part of the armoury of a would-be maritime power. The overseas campaigns of the early years of Henry VIII's reign had swiftly consumed whatever reserves of treasure his father may have left him and made him heavily dependent upon parliamentary supply. The high-handed methods of cardinal Wolsey had antagonised parliament and driven England to the verge of rebellion. Now the new chief minister, Cromwell, was eager to find a way to strengthen the authority of the crown by rescuing it from too great a dependence upon parliamentary taxation. The wealth of the monasteries would naturally catch his eye. The general reputation of the orders was low. There would be few to defend them from attack. The secular clergy were always jealous of the monks, and were more likely to rejoice at the destruction of the religious orders than to grieve over the loss of property to the church. Furthermore, the monasteries were the chief patrons of and gainers from pilgrimages and relics, and an attack on them would speed the suppression of such superstitions.

E

That Cromwell had the dissolution of the monasteries in mind from quite early on in his career in the king's service is made clear by a document[1] which probably dates from 1534 and details the most sweeping scheme for the conversion of ecclesiastical property to secular uses. Not only were the smaller religious houses to be expropriated, but the larger ones were to have their incomes pruned, and the bishops and other higher clergy were to be deprived of their endowments and put on fixed salaries. In the event, however, Cromwell's programme was a little more modest. The bishops he wisely left alone. It would have been gratuitous foolishness to have antagonised them at the same time as the religious orders. For the time being also the larger abbeys were left untouched. They had their champions in the parliamentary abbots who might readily accept a partial dissolution which did not affect their own houses, especially if it could be presented in the guise of a measure of reform, but would undoubtedly resist strenuously any frontal attack upon the religious orders as a whole. Whatever Cromwell's long-term plans may have been, the dissolution began as a modest campaign against the smaller and more defenceless abbeys. But for some years before the first open assault was launched, the ground was being prepared.

The Royal Headship and the Monasteries

Although the act of Supremacy did not pass through parliament until the autumn of 1534, the king had since 1531 been recognised by the English clergy as 'Supreme Head of the Church in England'. To many of the secular clergy this new title, with its famous qualifying clause 'in so far as the law of Christ allows', must have seemed largely a matter of words, but some of the English monks were soon to learn that the change in headship had practical and appreciable consequences. For many centuries some of the religious orders, notably the Cistercians, had enjoyed, by papal concession, the privilege of being exempt from the ordinary course of ecclesiastical discipline by the diocesan bishops, and were accustomed to regulate their own affairs, subject only to the overriding but seldom exercised authority of the pope. This privilege was also enjoyed individually by some of the older and more famous Benedictine houses. Exemption from episcopal visitation did not, however, mean exemption from all disciplinary oversight. The 'exempt' orders, as they were called,

[1] See L. Stone in *Bulletin of the Institute of Historical Research*, 1951.

appointed their own visitors who were probably more assiduous in the discharge of their duties than most diocesan bishops. In the case of orders organised on international lines, such as the Cistercians, the visitors were frequently foreigners to England, and the jurisdiction of these aliens was as objectionable to the new Supreme Head of the Church in England as that of the pope upon whose authority the privileges of the exempt orders rested. It was not long, therefore, before a change was made. On 10 April 1532 the king excluded from England the jurisdiction of the then visitor-general of the Cistercians and appointed a commission of five English Cistercian abbots to act in his place. Nor were these newly nominated visitors allowed to remain inactive. In the year of their appointment they descended upon Vaudey (Lincs.), and had to be reproved by their royal master for their excessive zeal. In the following year they were sent to investigate the alleged poisoning of the abbot of Holmcultram (Cumberland), and later in the same year they were required to supervise the deposition of the abbot of Rievaulx (Yorks.) and the election of his successor. This last incident, which is very well documented, is worth examining in some detail as it shows so clearly the lengths to which Thomas Cromwell, not yet the king's vicar-general, but already his chief minister and the prime director of government policy, was prepared to go to secure the election of his own candidate as abbot.

The story begins in April 1533 with a letter from the earl of Rutland, 'founder' and lay patron of the abbey, complaining of the conduct and reputation of the abbot, Edward Kirkby, and asking for an enquiry. Cromwell's immediate response was to send down a group of commissioners headed by the abbot of Fountains (one of the recently appointed Cistercian visitors)

> 'to enquire in due form of the living and order of the abbot . . . . and in case they found him of misorder and living, then by the order of the law and virtue of our said commission, to depose him'.

The abbot of Fountains was from the first unhappy about the legality of the whole proceeding, doubting whether a royal commission could give him authority to depose a fellow abbot without recourse to the normal disciplinary machinery of the Cistercian order. Indeed, as was said of him at the time, he cared too much for 'the rules of his religion' to be a very effective instrument of the will of the king's chief minister. After many delays and hesitations, therefore, he attempted to withdraw from the business altogether when, in August, Thomas Legh (later to be famous as one of the authors of the *Compendium Compertorum*) arrived at Rievaulx with instructions from Cromwell to press Kirkby to confess to the faults alleged against him, and to resign his office. Pressure from Legh soon produced the required result and the way seemed clear for a new election.

Unwilling to abandon all hope of securing the co-operation of the abbot of Fountains, Cromwell once again included him in the new commission to

'procure by all the lawful means and ways you can the convent to proceed to the election of a new abbot'.

But, as before, the abbot of Fountains managed to avoid the chief responsibility which fell this time to his fellow visitor and commissioner, the abbot of Byland. The latter reached Rievaulx in October, but soon found himself faced with a very difficult situation. Though he tried every means of persuasion at his command in an effort to prevail upon the monks to agree to the holding of an election, only five of the twenty-three brethren would give their unqualified approval to the course of action which he proposed. Four others were willing, somewhat reluctantly, and with various reservations, to proceed to an election if the visitor insisted, but the remaining fourteen were uncompromising in their resolute assertion that no election could take place because Kirkby had not been lawfully deposed, and was still abbot.

In reporting this state of affairs to Cromwell the abbot of Byland expressed the hope that he might now be discharged from a task which he had carried out to the best of his ability, but the king's minister, growing more confident of his power, was no longer content that his will should be thwarted by the legalistic scruples of Cistercian abbots and monks. The reply which he addressed to the two abbots of Byland and Fountains (who as fellow commissioners were equally responsible though only the first had been active) is justly famous as one of Cromwell's more stinging letters. He reminds the abbots that their task was to secure the election of a new abbot, and adds

'his Grace (i.e. the king) hath been advertised you have not heretofore endeavoured yourselves to the accomplishment of the same according to his said letters and commandment, whereof I marvel not a little that you would incur his high displeasure for the non-executing of the same' ending with a strict injunction to pursue the matter to its conclusion. Whether this letter had the desired effect, or whether the intervention of Thomas Legh was once again necessary, it is impossible to be quite certain, but the latter alternative seems the more likely as it was Legh who wrote to Cromwell in December to announce that the election had been duly completed, and the new abbot installed.

The Influence of the Crown

Chiefly significant in this long drawn-out affair is the ultimate triumph of the will of Cromwell, backed by the formidable authority of the crown, over all the hesitations and misgivings of the two visiting abbots and the direct opposition of the majority of the monks of Rievaulx. The full meaning of the royal headship was thus brought home to some of the more prominent men in the most important of the exempt orders, and Cromwell secured the election of his own candidate to the headship of an important abbey.

This Rievaulx election is not an isolated case, nor were the Cistercians the only order to be subjected to such pressures. Throughout the early years of his ascendancy Cromwell kept a careful and continuous eye on monastic affairs, and quite regularly put forward and secured the election of his own candidates to vacant abbacies. In the long run this interest in the internal affairs of the religious orders was to pay rich dividends. When, in 1538 and 1539, the heads of the larger abbeys were being persuaded to surrender the property of their houses to the crown, the fact that a considerable number of them owed their promotion to Cromwell's support in earlier years and were anxious now to retain his good opinion by readily co-operating in his schemes, must have speeded the process of the dissolution quite considerably. But we must not draw from this the conclusion that Cromwell necessarily had such long-term effects in mind when he interfered in abbatial elections in 1533 and 1534. He may at that time have been doing no more than indulging his taste for the exercise of patronage. Nor should it be thought that Cromwell was the first king's minister to interfere in the internal affairs of the monasteries in this way. Wolsey had done it before him, though by no means as frequently.

It was not only in the exercise of a controlling influence over elections that Cromwell, in the name of the crown, made his authority felt in the cloister. Another index of his increasing interest in monastic affairs is provided by the record of his activities on behalf of clients seeking leases, farms, stewardships and other profitable grants from the religious houses. The habit of sub-letting every species of monastic property from single tenements to whole manors and parsonages was not a new one, nor was the corresponding habit among laymen of petitioning abbots, priors and prioresses for such grants. What was to give the whole practice a very different aspect in the 1530s was the increasing frequency with which would-be lessors called to their assistance the name and influence of the king's chief minister. Here again we find that Wolsey had set his successor the example, but the full development of this sort of patronage did not come until 1532 and later when it was Cromwell who was in control.

Thus, in the years between the rise of Cromwell to power and the beginning of the dissolution, the religious orders in England were made to feel ever more firmly the hand of the government upon them, and the reality of the power of the Supreme Head of the English church. And yet, down to the summer of 1534, it was chiefly the larger and wealthier abbeys, which could dispense a profitable amount of patronage and provide their abbots with comfortable livings, which felt the effect of this increasing interest of the crown in their affairs. The smaller and poorer houses did not attract the same degree of attention, but even they could hardly have been entirely ignorant of the great changes that were taking place and of the important measures which were being discussed and adopted in parliament and convocation between 1529 and 1534.

The first act of the 'reformation parliament' to affect directly all the religious, both rich and poor alike, was the Succession act (25 Henry VIII c. 22), passed in the spring of 1534. With its requirements, and with the response of the monks to it, we have already dealt. The next session of parliament, in the autumn of the same year, saw the passage of the act of Supremacy (26 Henry VIII c. 1) which not only provided parliamentary confirmation for the king's new title, but expressly confirmed to him a general power to visit and correct abuses in the church, which, as we have seen he had already, more than two years previously, assumed and exercised in the case of the Cistercians. The power of the crown over the church was now made plain for all to see.

The Tenth and the Visitation

In the same session of parliament there also passed the First Fruits and Tenths act (26 Henry VIII c. 3) which imposed upon the whole clergy, both secular and monastic, a perpetual tax of one-tenth of their net annual income, together with the further obligation to surrender to the crown the first year's revenue from any new appointment. In order to ensure that this new tax should yield the maximum amount the act also provided for the appointment of commissioners to conduct a nation-wide survey of clerical incomes. In January 1535 these commissioners were duly appointed, and they spent the whole of the spring and most of the summer on their task. They were for the most part the usual agents of the crown in the shires, the local gentry and the higher clergy, but it is interesting to notice that a high proportion of the lay commissioners were men who were already, as stewards, receivers or bailiffs, involved in the administration of the estates of the larger monasteries. Many of them were to be purchasers of abbey lands after the dissolution. Some of them were also to act as commissioners for the suppression, and thus to be involved intimately in almost every stage of the process of dissolution. But for the time being, however, their task was not only to record for the benefit of the government the value of every bishopric, deanery, archdeaconry, vicarage and chaplaincy, but also to produce a very ample and entirely up-to-date account of the income of every religious house, and the sources from which it came.

It was, presumably, after studying the returns of these Tenths commissioners that an income of £200 a year was chosen by the authors of the Suppression act as the criterion to separate the smaller abbeys which were to be dissolved from the larger which were to be spared. They could see from the figures before them that to adopt this dividing line would provide the crown with a comfortable endowment without antagonising any of the more powerful religious interests. Thus we can, in a sense, regard the First Fruits and Tenths act as a necessary preliminary to any programme of dissolution, or even as the first stage in the process of suppression. Before any realistic plan for a partial dissolution of the religious orders could be decided upon it was necessary to have adequate and up-to-date information about the wealth of the monasteries. This the Tenths commissioners supplied.[2]

[2] A sample extract from their returns will be found in the appendix to this chapter.

The next step was to prepare the case against the monks and nuns. This was done, as we have seen (Chapter 3) by Cromwell, in his capacity as king's vicar-general (a position to which he was appointed in January 1535) commissioning visitors and dispatching them upon a tour of as many religious houses as they could manage to visit in the time available. It is noteworthy that on this occasion the local gentry were not employed. The visitors were all Cromwell's men, picked in the knowledge that they would perform efficiently what was required of them. Richard Layton, one of the chosen few, clearly knew what was expected of him when he wrote to ask Cromwell to send him and Thomas Legh to visit the northern province.

> 'There is neither monastery, cell, priory nor any other religious house in the north but either Dr. Legh or I have familiar acquaintance within 10 or 12 miles of it so that no knavery can be hid from us in that country'

and so no other applicant for appointment as visitor would be

> 'so trusty, true and faithful . . . doing all things diligently for your purpose'.

And, as we saw in the last chapter, Layton, Legh and the other visitors did not disappoint their master, and served his purpose very well.

APPENDIX: AN EXTRACT FROM THE *VALOR ECCLESIASTICUS*

(From the Record Commission edition of 1810–34, vol. III, pp. 73–4. The original is in Latin which is so rigorously contracted as to be almost in a form of shorthand. As the purpose of including this extract is to show the kind of information which can be found in the *Valor* and not to set the reader an exercise in extension and translation, an English paraphrase is used throughout. For similar reasons the roman numerals of the original have been replaced by their arabic equivalents. Maxstoke, having considerably less than £200 clear annual income, was dissolved in 1536, the prior getting a pension of £13 : 6 : 8. The proportion of the income of this priory which came from spiritual sources (56%) is untypically high. The entries (under the heading of 'Alms' and in the totals) which are given in italic type, have been deleted in the original because the amounts claimed, although recorded by the commissioners, were disallowed by the Court of First Fruits and Tenths.)

DIOCESE OF COVENTRY AND LICHFIELD
DEANERY OF ARDEN
Priory of Maxstoke
Dominus William Dicons prior

Income received from churches appropriated to the priory

In tithes and oblations from the parish church of Maxstoke in the county of Warwick	£3 : 13 : 8	
From the farm of the rectory of Shustoke in the same county	£6 : 3 : 4	
From the farm of the tithes of Bentley in the same county	£2 : 13 : 4	
From the farm of the rectory of Tanworth in the same county	£3 : 13 : 4	
From the farm of the rectory of Long Itchington in the same county	£16 : 13 : 4	
From the farm of the rectory of Fillongley in the same county	£8 : 0 : 0	
From the farm of the rectory of Aston Cantlow in the same county	£24 : 0 : 0	
From the farm of the rectory of Yardley in the county of Worcester	£8 : 0 : 0	
TOTAL		£72 : 17 : 0

Fixed rents

From Maxstoke in the county of Warwick	3 : 6½	
From Solihull in the same county	5 : 0	
TOTAL		8 : 6½

Income from lands, tenements, meadows, grazing and pasture

From lands and tenements in Maxstoke in the county of Warwick	£11 : 0 : 9	
From certain lands in Shustoke in the same county	8	
From lands and tenements in Long Itchington in the same county	£7 : 4 : 9	
From lands and tenements in Fillongley in the same county	£3 : 14 : 0	
From lands and tenements in Aston Cantlow in the same county	£1 : 10 : 0	
From lands and tenements in divers other villages in the county of Warwick for the obits of divers benefactors	£1 : 6 : 0	
From lands and tenements in Yardley in the county of Worcester	£8 : 0 : 0	
From lands and tenements in Dunton Bassett in the county of Leicester	£10 : 0 : 0	
TOTAL		£42 : 16 : 2

Demesne lands reserved for the use of the Guesthouse

From such of the demesne as is not let but is reserved for the use of the guesthouse, together with the grazing of the park of the priory, and the meadows, and all the other demesne lands, by estimation, yearly

TOTAL £12 : 0 : 0

Sale of woods and profits of the court

From the sale of wood and the profits of the court by estimation of the commissioners and others in an average year

TOTAL £1 : 10 : 0

SUM TOTAL OF ALL THE INCOME OF THE PRIORY £129 : 11 : 8½

ALLOWANCES

Rents paid

To the abbot and convent of Kenilworth 3 : 0
To the heirs of Lord de Clynton for lands in Maxstoke 10 : 11

TOTAL 13 : 11

Paid in pensions, augmentations, procurations and synodals

Annual pension to the bishop of
Worcester from the churches of

Tanworth	£1 : 6 : 8	
Yardley	£1 : 0 : 0	
Aston Cantlow	£1 : 0 : 0	

and to the prior and convent of the cathedral monastery there for a similar pension from the the same churches £2 : 13 : 4

in all £6 : 0 : 0

Annual pension to the abbot and convent of the monastery of Kenilworth from the church of Tanworth £1 : 10 : 8

Annual pension to the bishop of Coventry and Lichfield from the churches of Fillongley Shu-stokc and Maxstoke £1 : 0 : 0
and to the archdeacon of Coventry from the same churches 14 : 2

in all £1 : 14 : 2

Pension to the archdeacon of Worcester from the church of Tanworth 8 : 5½

In annual augmentation of the stipend of the perpetual vicar of Fillongley	£1 :	0 :	0
In annual augmentation of the rectory of Packington Pigott		10 :	0
Stipend of the perpetual vicar of Maxstoke	£5 :	6 :	8
Stipend of a priest celebrating Mass weekly in the chapel of Bentley	£2 :	13 :	4
Paid on the occasion of the bishop's visitation £4 : 1 : 8 every third year, i.e. per annum	£1 :	7 :	2½
TOTAL	£20 :	10 :	6

Alms

Alms distributed daily to the poor in the priory, i.e. a loaf, a flagon of ale and a dish of food at a cost of 4d a day, and prescribed by the will of the first founder	£6 :	1 :	8
Alms distributed on Maundy Thursday to the poor within the priory and at the gates, in money, bread, drink and herrings	£4 :	0 :	0
Stipends of two chaplains celebrating Mass weekly in the Lady Chapel of the priory on the foundation of Ade Overton	*£3 :*	*6 :*	*8*
Alms given for the soul of William de Clynton one of the founders of the priory, and distributed weekly to one of the canons saying Mass for the soul of the same, per week 12d, per annum	*£2 :*	*12 :*	*0*
TOTAL	£10 :	1 :	8

Fees and wages of officers

Sir Edward Ferrers, chief steward	£3 :	0 :	0
John Brown, receiver general	£2 :	0 :	0
William Pynnok, auditor	£1 :	6 :	8
John Hopkins, bailiff of Long Itchington	£1 :	0 :	0
Griffith Thomas, bailiff of Yardley		13 :	4
John Preston, bailiff of Maxstoke	£2 :	0 :	0
John Launt, bailiff in Dunton Bassett		13 :	4
TOTAL	£10 :	13 :	4

SUM TOTAL OF ALL THE ALLOWANCES OF THE PRIORY	£41 :	19 :	5
And so the clear value, making all allowances, is	*£81 :*	*13 :*	*7½*

Adding in the £3 : 6 : 8 for the stipend of the two chaplains celebrating Mass in the Lady Chapel of the priory on the foundation of Ade Overton and the £2 : 12 : 0 for the stipend of a canon celebrating Mass for the soul of William de Clynton and the sum of £81 : 13 : 7½, the clear value of the said priory comes to £87 : 12 : 3½

Of which the TENTH part is £8 : 15 : 2¾

5

Dissolution by Statute

On 4 February 1536 the 'reformation parliament' which had stood prorogued since 18 December 1534, reassembled for what was to be the last session of its unprecedentedly long life. Some time between then and 14 April, when it was finally dissolved, it gave its approval to the act for the dissolution of the lesser monasteries (27 Henry VIII c. 28) Because of the fragmentary nature of the records of parliamentary proceedings at that date we cannot be very much more precise about the exact days upon which the act passed through its various stages, but, in accordance with the constitutional convention of the time, it was deemed to have come into force on the first day of the session in which it was passed, so that in law the fixed assets of all the lesser religious houses affected by the act were transferred to the crown on 4 February, at least three and a half weeks before Richard Layton and Thomas Legh had finished their visitation of the northern province. In fact, however, we can infer from contemporary letters that the dissolution act was not presented to parliament until about the end of the second week in March, so that there was just about time for the results of the northern visitation to be added to the dossier of monastic sins which the government had been engaged in preparing since the previous autumn, before the case against the religious orders had to be stated in public.

Just exactly what use was made of the *Compendium Compertorum*, and of similar reports from other royal visitors, at the time when the act was under consideration in parliament, we once again cannot say for certain, but of two things we can be reasonably sure. In the first place the opportunity to blacken the reputation of the religious orders by revealing some measure of the extent of the iniquity which the visitors claimed to have found was not lost. Latimer's testimony, given years later, to the effect that there was a great spontaneous outcry against the monks when their enormities were first revealed to parliament, may have been coloured by what he then knew of the years that followed, but the act itself did claim that its condemnation of the lesser abbeys was based upon the findings of the king's 'late visitation' as well as other 'sundry credible informations'. Yet we can be equally sure that the *Compendium* itself was not laid before the houses without some careful preliminary editing. As it stood it would hardly have suited the government's immediate purpose which was to establish that it was chiefly, indeed exclusively, the smaller religious houses which were incurably devoted to 'vicious, carnal and abominable living'. The *Compendium*, as we have seen, tended if anything to present the larger abbeys in the worse light, and so any public readings from it would have had to have been very carefully selected.

We should not, however, imagine that any very subtle propaganda campaign nor yet any substantial political pressures were needed to secure the fairly ready acceptance by both houses of parliament of this dissolution act, for it was, when properly understood, quite a moderate measure. This point will best be made clear by a closer look at the terms of the act itself.

The Terms of the Act

The lengthy preamble with which the act opens (see appendix to this chapter) is, like the preambles to so many Tudor statutes, largely government propaganda designed to demonstrate the pressing need to take some such action as in fact the act prescribes. As we have already seen in Chapter 3, it justified the proposed suppressions on the good moral grounds that all the smaller monasteries and nunneries were irredeemably sunk in iniquity which the traditional disciplinary machinery of the church had proved powerless to eradicate. And so

'it is, and shall be, much more to the pleasure of Almighty God and for the honour of this his realm, that the possessions of such spiritual religious houses, now being spent spoiled and wasted for increase and maintenance of sin, should be used and converted to better uses, and the unthrifty religious persons so spending the same to be compelled to reform their lives'.

This latter purpose was to be achieved by transferring the monks canons and nuns from the dissolved priories to the greater houses of their orders where

'thanks be to God, religion is right well kept and observed'.

The precise nature of the 'better uses' to which the endowments of the suppressed houses were to be put was nowhere stated, and the only restriction placed upon the king's freedom to do what he liked with the properties which he was about to acquire was the very vague and general stipulation that he should

'do and use therewith . . . to the pleasure of Almighty God and to the honour and profit of this realm'.

The religious houses whose property was thus to come into the king's hands so that it might be put to such unspecified 'better uses' were all those

'monasteries, priories and other religious houses of monks, canons and nuns'

whose net annual income had been assessed by the commissioners for the royal Tenth at less than £200. How many of them were there? Not perhaps so many as at first sight might be thought. It is important to notice that the phrase 'monks, canons and nuns' does not include the friars who had at this time no less than 187 houses in England and Wales. More firmly devoted to the ideal of apostolic poverty than the older established monastic orders, the friars had more effectively resisted the temptation to acquire the wealth and comfort which a permanent endowment so often brought. In theory they were still propertyless, dependent upon the alms of the people to whom they preached and ministered. In practice, in the towns in which they lived and worked, they sometimes owned quite valuable central sites upon which they had built substantial houses and churches. The Dominicans' house in London (Blackfriars) was, for example, large enough to provide comfortable accommodation for a meeting of parliament. And yet, however extensive or imposing the buildings which the friars possessed, these were practically their only assets. Few of them had any endowments capable of being taxed or seized by a financially embarrassed government. They were not, therefore, expressly included in the catalogue of clergy required to pay the new royal tax of the Tenth, and most of their houses escaped the attentions of the Tenths commissioners. Only eighteen friaries appear in the *Valor Ecclesiasticus* and the wealthiest of these is the Carmelite house in Northampton which was rated at £10 10s. 0d. per annum The average income of the eighteen is, however, only £4 10s. 0d. There was clearly little to be gained by dissolving the mendicant orders, and their omission from the suppression act is quite deliberate. When the friaries did eventually come into the possession of the crown in 1538 and 1539, it was by virtue of their own surrenders and not by force of the dissolution act of 1536.

The Moderation of the Act

Deducting the friaries from the total number of religious houses in England and Wales, we are left with about 638 houses of monks, canons and nuns, of which 419, or very nearly two-thirds, had been assessed for the Tenth at less than £200 a year, and therefore came within the category of small abbeys as defined by the dissolution act. But by no means all of these were dissolved. In the first place only independent houses were covered by the act. Cells of larger houses, that is to say small priories which did not possess the power to regulate their own affairs but were merely dependent offshoots of larger establishments, were, for the purpose of the act, regarded as parts of their respective mother houses and shared their fate. In practice, this meant that such cells were left untouched as it was normally only the greater abbeys which had acquired or created such dependencies. No fewer than ninety-two of these cells must therefore be removed from the list of small religious houses affected by the dissolution act, reducing the total to 327.

A further seventeen small priories belonging to the exclusively English order of St. Gilbert of Sempringham were also exempted *en bloc* from the operation of the act for reasons at which we can only guess, and by a process which is not at all clear. There is no specific mention of the Gilbertines in the dissolution act itself, nor is there extant any formal grant of exemption by royal letters patent as provided for by the clause which empowered the king, at his pleasure to

'ordain and declare by his letters patent under his great seal that such of the said religious houses which his highness shall not be disposed to have suppressed nor dissolved by authority of this act shall still continue remain and be in the same body corporate and in the said essential estate quality and condition . . . as they were before the making of this act'.

However, the instructions which were issued to the commissioners appointed to put the suppression act into force required them not to touch the Gilbertine priories save to send their priors up to the capital to learn the king's pleasure concerning their houses. No Gilbertine priory was in fact suppressed in 1536, the king's pleasure being, apparently, that they should all for the time being be spared. When the Gilbertine houses eventually fell they fell like the friaries and the larger abbeys, by making individual surrenders of their properties to the crown, and not by virtue of any act of parliament.

Why were the Gilbertines thus favoured in 1536? It so happened that the Master of the order was at that time Robert Holgate who enjoyed the confidence and favour of Thomas Cromwell, and was soon to be promoted to the bishopric of Llandaff and the presidency of the Council of the North. It is generally assumed that it was his personal influence with Cromwell which secured this special treatment for the order of which he was the head. It has also been suggested that to have dissolved the Gilbertine houses at this stage would have created a difficult problem in finding alternative accommodation for the many nuns from the double houses of the order who would be unlikely to want to abandon the conventual life. However, this particular problem was not exclusive to the Gilbertines. It affected equally acutely all the orders of nuns, as we shall see, and yet no other order was granted a similar wholesale exemption from suppression.

Excluding the Gilbertines from the count, the number of small priories affected by the dissolution act is further reduced to 310, a little over one-third of all the religious houses in the kingdom. The act contained, however, as we have seen, a clause empowering the king to grant exemption from its terms to any abbey or priory he might chose to favour, and in the end no fewer than sixty-seven small houses escaped suppression in this way. The total number of priories actually suppressed in 1536 was therefore only 243, or approximately three out of every ten religious houses throughout the country. When it is remembered further that the suppressed houses were the smallest and least significant of their kind, we can begin to see the dissolution act in its proper perspective. It was by no means a frontal assault upon the religious orders. Had no other suppressions followed those of 1536 we should probably not now regard the act as particularly significant. We might indeed defend it as a reasonable measure of reorganisation whereby the vacant places in the larger abbeys were filled up and the surplus wealth of the orders released for other purposes. We must not therefore expect to find the Lords and Commons in 1536 raising any very substantial objection to the passage of the act, or needing much persuasion before giving it their assent.

The Protection of Interests

But it was not only the moderate scope of the dissolution act which made it acceptable even to the parliamentary abbots in the house of Lords, whose abbeys were, of course, too wealthy to be in any danger from it. Another noticeable feature of the act which must have eased its passage is the care which it took to protect from loss all those who had any interest in or claim upon the properties of the monasteries to be dissolved. Not only did the crown take over the assets of these houses, it also took over their debts and other obligations. The fees of lay officials were still to be paid. The rights of annuitants, corrodians and lessees of monastic properties were fully protected, and even the rather vague prerogatives of founders were preserved by a last minute proviso.

The inhabitants of the suppressed houses were also carefully provided for. Abbots, priors and prioresses, who, having once ruled over their convents, could not be expected readily to accept a subordinate status in another house, were to be granted pensions by the king 'of his most excellent charity'. The rank and file of the religious were to be transferred to the surviving houses of their orders whose heads were required by the act to take them in. If, however, they did not like the prospect of continuing the monastic life in a strange cloister where their presence might well be resented as an intrusion, they could apply for a dispensation (known as a 'capacity') which would release them from the specifically monastic vows of poverty and obedience, and would enable them to embark upon a fresh career in the secular world outside the cloister. In this case they would also be given 'some convenient charity', a small gratuity to help them on their way.

An attempt was also made to protect the interests of the farm hands, domestic servants and local paupers who were employed by or depended upon the charity of the priories which were to be closed down. All future occupants of these houses, farmers renting their

F

property from the crown, or purchasers of their sites and demesne lands, were required, under penalty, to

'maintain an honest continual house and household'

and to plough as much land as previously had been ploughed, so that neither hospitality nor tillage should decay, and local unemployment be kept to a minimum. It is indeed difficult to think of any vested interest which the dissolution act did not do its best to protect. The transfer to the crown of the properties of these small priories was to be effected with the minimum of disturbance to the lives of all concerned.

On the other hand it is equally clear from the provisions of the act, and from the way in which these were later put into effect, that the government was determined that the policy of providing compensation for all should be carried out with the minimum of expense, so that the maximum financial benefit might be assured to the crown from its newly acquired properties. The undertaking to continue the payment of fees and annuities was probably the most costly commitment, but it was also politically the most necessary, as so many of the country gentry whose influence predominated in the house of Commons and had therefore to be respected, were recipients of payments of this kind. But care was also taken to see that the crown's future outgoings on this score were kept to a minimum. In an attempt to guard against fraudulent last-minute grants of excessive fees or annuities and unduly favourable leases, it was provided by the act that all such grants which had been made within one year before its passing were to be subject to careful scrutiny by government officials before the crown would honour their terms.

The pensions paid to the abbots and prioresses were not politically so important and, in the circumstances, were quite generous. They were, however, made roughly proportionate to the revenues of the individual houses, so that whereas the abbot of Sawley, a Cistercian house rated at £147, got the modest, but comfortable, sum of £20 a year, the prioress of the little nunnery of Ellerton (Yorks.), which was worth only £13, had to be content with £3. Compensation for the rank and file of the monks and nuns cost the government least of all. Those who opted for transfer to another house became a charge on the revenues of that establishment. Those who chose capacities were presumed to have rejected of their own free will the offer of an assured future in another cloister, and so could be quite justly dismissed with a modest once-for-all payment in the region of £1 or 30*s*. to tide them over the period of adjustment to whatever new career they might have in mind. The responsibility for maintaining local employment and hospitality was placed firmly upon the shoulders of lessees and grantees.

The Transfer of the Dispossessed

So much for the terms of the act. Of all its clauses the one providing for the transfer of the dispossessed religious to other houses was the one which was to create the most difficulty when the time came to put the act into force. But the care which the government nevertheless took to ensure that no one who really wanted to continue the religious life was prevented from so doing is worth noting because of the significant inferences about government policy which we can draw from it. If, in 1536, it had already been decided that the monastic orders should be abolished altogether, if, that is to say, the dissolution act was from the very beginning intended to be no more than the first stage in the fulfilment of a more ambitious programme of total dissolution, it would hardly have been worth the government's while to have devoted so much time and energy to finding new homes for the former inhabitants of the first batch of houses to be dissolved. In the later suppressions, those that took place in 1538–40, the evicted religious were given no option but to accept a government pension as compensation for the loss of their accustomed living. Those who were then awarded these pensions included all those monks and nuns from the smaller houses who had accepted transfer to larger abbeys in 1536. This latter group were thus displaced for the second time in the comparatively short period of two or three years. Had the later suppressions been already in contemplation in 1536 it would surely have been simpler to have awarded pensions to all from the very beginning. The fact that the option of transfer was made available in 1536 does seem thus to indicate that initially no more than a partial dissolution was intended.

Having decided to dissolve the lesser abbeys, and to cut the cost of compensation to a minimum by offering places in surviving houses to those whose cloisters were to be closed, the government's next problem was to ensure that a sufficient supply of such places was in fact available to meet whatever demand there might be. The nature of the provisions incorporated in the dissolution act to deal with this problem reveals the government's appreciation of the proportions which it might attain. Until all the religious in the small houses covered by the act had been consulted about their preferences the government could not know how many would be content to accept a capacity and how many would prefer to take up the offer of transfer. The number asking for transfers might well be large, so large as to make it impossible for the undissolved abbeys to absorb them all. It might thus be necessary to save some of the smaller houses from suppression in order to provide a sufficient number of places. And so the act empowered the crown to grant special exemption from suppression to as many of the smaller abbeys as it might choose.

Properly understood, this discretionary clause, under which in the end more than one-fifth of the smaller religious houses were saved from immediate suppression, should be regarded as an integral part of the suppression act and as a necessary consequence of the policy of permitting the evicted religious to transfer to other cloisters, and not, as some authorities have tended to represent it, merely as a money-raising after-thought. It is, of course, true that thirty-two of the sixty-seven exempted houses did pay substantial sums by way of 'fines for continuance', but the other thirty-five paid nothing and got their exemption free. There are also hints, here and there, as in the report of the suppression commissioners for Lancashire, that the monks and nuns of the threatened houses were sometimes asked how much they would be prepared to pay to save their cloister from suppression. Undoubtedly there was money to be made out of grants of exemption, and the government was quite prepared to make it. But to admit this is not to admit that the prime reason for the insertion of the exemption clause in the act was financial. The willingness or ability of particular houses to pay for the privilege of exemption perhaps determined in some cases which convents in any particular district survived and which did not, but in every district where any substantial number of the monks or nuns affected by the act wished to remain in their habits some exemptions would have to be granted, whether or not any money was forthcoming in the form of fines. The prime purpose of the exemption clause was to enable the government to solve the potential accommodation problem. The raising of money by fines was an incidental bonus.

The Accommodation Problem

How great in fact did this accommodation problem prove to be? The paucity of the evidence precludes us from offering more than a partial answer. When the suppression commissioners were set to work in the spring and early summer of 1536 the tasks which they were required to perform included the noting down and reporting back of the preference for capacity or transfer expressed by every monk, canon and nun in the houses affected by the dissolution act. We know sufficient about the way in which the commissioners worked to be reasonably certain that they did indeed carry out this part of their instructions as faithfully as any other, but the results of their enquiries are available for only seventy-eight houses, or about one-quarter of the total number with which they were concerned. And yet these seventy-eight may be taken as a fairly representative selection of the whole, for they lie in six widely scattered regions which included such contrasting counties as Surrey, Wiltshire, Norfolk and Yorkshire. Of the total of 576 religious persons living in these seventy-eight houses in 1536, 404, or appoximately 70%, had no desire to abandon their accustomed way of life, and asked to be transferred to larger abbeys. This general figure conceals, however, wide regional variations. In Norfolk the proportion desiring transfer was as low as 25%. In Surrey and Sussex it was 28%. On the other hand, in Yorkshire, at the fourteen houses for which figures are available, 95%, and in Leicestershire and Warwickshire 83% of the religious wanted to remain in the cloister.

There is also a significant difference between the response of the monks and canons and that of the nuns to this question about their preferences for the future. For the men a capacity had its attractions. Released from the cloister they could expect to find, without too much difficulty, alternative employment as parish or chantry priests, as private chaplains or as clerks in royal or noble service. For the women, however, life outside the cloister had no such attractions. Few families would welcome the return to dependent status of a daughter whom they thought had been comfortably provided for in some nunnery. Such women, though released by their capacity from their vows of poverty and obedience, were still bound by that of chastity and could not seek security in marriage, and, outside marriage, the sixteenth century offered few careers for women. It need not surprise us therefore to discover that the overall figure of a 70% preference for transfer rather than capacity breaks down into one as high as 85% for women and one of only 58% for men. In the figure for women the regional variations are even more marked than they are in the overall figures. In Yorkshire only one nun out of 105, and in Hampshire, Wiltshire and Gloucestershire only one nun out of fifty-nine, asked to have a capacity. In Norfolk, on the other hand, less than a quarter of the nuns wanted to stay in the cloister, and in Sussex, the only two nuns consulted both asked for release from their vows.

The influence which the preferences of the religious themselves could exercise in determining how many small houses in any one district were exempted from suppression is most easily seen in the area supervised by the Augmentations' receiver for Yorkshire.[1] Though the figures just quoted cover only twelve of the twenty nunneries in the district, it is clear that the nuns in the other eight houses must have been just as contented with their lot as all their sisters, for in the end only seven of the Yorkshire nunneries were actually suppressed in 1536 while thirteen were granted exemption. Yet none of these latter paid any fine for the privilege. It was simply the case that they had to be spared to house all the many nuns who wanted to remain in the cloister.

Such a large number of exemptions in a single district is, however, exceptional. No other Augmentations' district had more than nine, and the average was more like four. The Yorkshire figure is probably the product of two special conditions, the one peculiar to the women's orders, the other to Yorkshire. As a general rule, applicable throughout England and Wales, the nunneries were smaller and poorer than the men's houses. Indeed, less than a score of nunneries throughout the whole kingdom had annual incomes greater than the critical figure of £200, and none of these was north of Trent. If, therefore, the 1536 act had been applied without exception, there would have been no nunneries left in Yorkshire at all, however many or few nuns wished to remain in their habits. Some exemptions would almost certainly have had to be granted.

In the second place the Yorkshire nunneries were not just small, but very small. The richest of them, Swine, was valued at only £82 a year.

[1] For a fuller examination of this point see G. W. O. Woodward, 'The Exemption from Suppression of Certain Yorkshire Priories' in *English Historical Review* (1961).

Only seven of them had more than £30 a year, and six had less than £20. Such poorly endowed convents could not very easily take in more than one or two additional nuns, and so, if any substantial proportion of the Yorkshire nuns wanted, as it seems that they did, to continue to live the religious life, a considerable number of these humble convents would have to be spared to provide housing for them all.

Capacities and Exemptions

In the case of the men's houses in Yorkshire this sort of problem did not arise. There were several large abbeys in the shire which together were well able to absorb most of the monks and canons from smaller houses who did not want capacities and so all but two of the lesser monasteries in the shire could be suppressed. The two exceptions were special cases. One was the Charterhouse at Hull. Although there was another, and larger, Carthusian house in Yorkshire, Mount Grace, the peculiar arrangement of the cloisters of that order, with their separate house and garden for each monk made it difficult to take in additional men at short notice, so that the Mount Grace and Hull communities could not easily be merged. The other exempted house was Grosmont, the sole remaining representative of the Grandimontine order in England. Its exemption is something of a mystery, or perhaps just an example of administrative incompetence, for the monks there had shown no great love for the conventual life, and had all asked for capacities to release them from their vows.

In no other part of the country is the relationship between the choice of the religious between capacity and transfer and the incidence of exemptions from suppression so clear as it is in Yorkshire, though it can generally be dimly discerned. In Norfolk, where only a quarter of all the religious asked for transfer, and in Surrey and Sussex, where the proportion opting for transfer was little larger, there were no exemptions at all. In Leicestershire and Warwickshire, where more than four fifths of the monks and nuns wanted to remain in religion, four exemptions were granted. In Hampshire, Wiltshire and Gloucestershire, where only one nun was prepared to accept a capacity, we should not be surprised to find that two out of the five small nunneries were spared from suppression. The percentage of men in this area who wished to remain in their orders was, however, substantially lower, and there was a sufficient number of larger houses available to receive them, so that no small monasteries were exempted there.

Taken over the whole of the kingdom the number of small religious houses to be granted exemption from suppression amounted to more than one in five of the total affected by the act of 1536. Clearly the smooth working of the scheme of transfer depended upon the power of the crown to grant such exemptions, and the fact that so many exemptions were granted is very revealing. It shows that the government did not really believe that all the smaller religious houses were the dens of vice which the preamble to the suppression act so unhesitatingly declared them to be, and had no intention just yet of abolishing the religious orders altogether. The dissolution act of 1536 should not be regarded as the first stage of a carefully planned attack upon English monasticism as a whole, but rather (despite the violent language of its preamble) as a moderate measure of reorganisation and economy, designed to release some surplus property for secular purposes while permitting the monks and nuns to continue to play a large part in the life of the nation.

APPENDIX:
THE PREAMBLE TO THE SUPPRESSION ACT

(From *Statutes of the Realm*, vol. III, p. 575. The spelling has been modernised. Although excerpts from both the preamble and the act itself are to be found in many works, the full text is rarely quoted. As the preamble is the fullest statement of the government case against the monasteries it is given here *in extenso* to assist the reader in forming his own judgment about the validity of that case.)

27 HENRY VIII Chapter 28

AN act whereby all religious houses of monks canons and nuns which may not dispend manors lands tenements and hereditaments above the clear yearly value of £200 are given to the King's Highness, his heirs and successors for ever.

Forasmuch as manifest sin, vicious carnal and abominable living, is daily used and committed amongst the little and small abbeys priories and other religious houses of monks canons and nuns, where the congregation of such religious persons is under the number of twelve persons, whereby the governors of such religious houses and their convents spoil destroy consume and utterly waste, as well their churches monasteries priories principal houses farms granges lands tenements and hereditaments, as the ornaments of their churches and their goods and chattels, to the high displeasure of Almighty God, slander of good religion and to the great infamy of the King's Highness and the realm if redress should not be had thereof; and albeit that many continual visitations hath been heretofore had by the space of two hundred years and more, for an honest and charitable reformation of such unthrifty carnal and abominable living, yet nevertheless little or none amendment is hitherto had, but their vicious living shamelessly increaseth and augmenteth, and by a cursed custom so rooted and infested that a great multitude of the religious persons in such small houses do rather choose to rove abroad in apostacy than to conform them to the observation of good religion; so that without such small houses be utterly suppressed and the religious persons therein committed to great and honourable monasteries of religion in this realm, where they may be compelled to live religiously for reformation of their lives, there can else be no reformation in this behalf: IN CONSIDERATION whereof the King's most royal Majesty being supreme head in earth under God of the Church of England, daily finding and devising the increase advancement and exaltation of true doctrine and virtue in the said Church, to the only glory and honour of God and the total extirpation and destruction of vice and sin, having knowledge that the premises be true, as well by the comperts of his late visitations as by sundry credible informations, considering also that divers and great solemn monasteries of this realm wherein, thanks be to God, religion is right well kept and observed, be destitute of such full numbers of religious persons as they ought and may keep, hath thought good that a plain declaration should be made of the premises as well to the Lords spiritual and temporal as to other his loving subjects the Commons in this present Parliament assembled; whereupon the said Lords and Commons by a great deliberation finally be resolved that it is and shall be much more to the pleasure of Almighty God and for the honour of this His realm that the possessions of such spiritual religious houses, now being spent spoiled and wasted for increase and maintenance of sin, should be used and converted to better uses, and the unthrifty religious persons so spending the same be compelled to reform their lives; And thereupon most humbly desire the King's Highness that it may be enacted by authority of this present parliament that his Majesty shall have and enjoy to him and to his heirs for ever all and singular such monasteries priories and other religious houses of monks canons and nuns of what kinds or diversities of habits rules or orders so ever they be called or named, which have not in lands and tenements rents tithes portions and other hereditaments above the clearly yearly value of two hundred pounds, etc.

6

The Suppression Commissioners at Work

In the session of parliament which saw the dissolution act become law there also passed an 'Act establishing the court of Augmentations'. This new government office was set up specifically for the purpose of supervising the transfer to the crown of the properties and possessions of the dissolved religious houses and administering them thereafter. The regular staff of Augmentations consisted of the chancellor, treasurer, attorney and solicitor who supervised the work of the department in Westminster, seventeen particular receivers, each responsible for collecting the proceeds of dissolution and administering the estates of the dissolved abbeys in his own district, and ten auditors who checked the receivers' accounts and lent a hand wherever necessary. Besides these principal officers Augmentations also employed a staff of clerks and a whole host of local bailiffs and collectors who were responsible to the receivers for the administration of particular estates. The warrants appointing the officers, receivers and auditors of the new court were issued on 24 April 1536, ten days after the dissolution of the parliament which had created it.

The Commissioners and Their Instructions

On the same day the work of dissolution was set on foot by the appointment of commissioners in every shire to survey the lands, goods and cattle of all the religious houses covered by the suppression act. The men appointed to carry out this important task were, for the most part, those tried agents of the Tudor crown, the local gentry, but of the five or six commissioners in each district one was invariably the newly appointed Augmentations' receiver for that district and another was one of the Augmentations' auditors. It is also worthy of note that in each case the terms of the commission specified a quorum of three, of which the receiver and the auditor were to be two. This meant, in effect, that the bulk of the work, and there was a considerable amount to do, was done by the staff of Augmentations itself with the local gentry being called upon merely to provide some semblance of local participation in the proceedings.

Most of the commissioners began work right away. In Northamptonshire they had almost finished the first part of their task by 12 May. In Lincolnshire, where there were many more houses to be attended to, they were nevertheless well on the way towards completion by 1 June. The instructions issued for their guidance were clear and specific, with the consequence that they all worked to a similar pattern. They were provided, at the outset, with a list of all the religious houses in their district which had been assessed at less than £200 a year by the commissioners for the Tenth in the previous year. These had all to be visited in turn.

On arrival at each house the commissioners were first to show the abbot, prior or prioress a copy of the suppression statute and of their own commission so that there should be no doubt about the authority upon which they were acting. They were then to scrutinise the deeds and muniments of the house in order to establish to what order it belonged and whether it was an independent house or a dependent cell. This preliminary scrutiny was important, for upon its findings the immediate fate of the priory might well depend. Houses of the Gilbertine order were, as we have seen (above, p. 68), to be left alone for the time being. In other cases individual priories were also successful in claiming exemption. The Augustinian canons of Beeston (Norfolk), for example, by pretending that they were friars, escaped suppression until 1538. The monks of the Benedictine house of Binham in the same county likewise postponed the dissolution of their house for two years by claiming that it was a cell of the great abbey of St. Albans, though this was not in fact true. On the other hand the prior of Brooke (Rutland), who was the only inhabitant of his house, seems to have been eager to end the monotony of his isolation, for he successfully claimed that his was an independent priory and therefore covered by the dissolution act, when it could as easily have been claimed as a cell of Kenilworth.

The Supervision

In those cases where no valid claim to immunity could be made the commissioners would next require the monks or nuns to give up to them the common seal of the priory. This was something more than a symbolic surrender of authority to the representatives of the crown, it was also a means of guaranteeing the preservation of the priory's property more or less intact until such a time as the crown could enter into full possession. Without its seal to authenticate transactions no convent could sell or lease lands, grant annuities or corrodies, or create new offices. The dissolution act had bound the king to respect all grants and bargains already made under convent seal. This, then, was a way of ensuring that no more could be made. The opportunities for the monks and nuns to make gifts and grants to their friends and neighbours in anticipation of their eventual suppression were, by this simple action considerably restricted.

For the rest, the commissioners' work at this stage (the stage which they themselves described as that of the 'supervision' of the priories in their commission), was restricted to the collection of information. They were required to compile a complete survey of all sources of income, whether from lands, tithes or offerings, and a comprehensive inventory of all movable property, including not only altar plate and valuable jewels (which were to be put in 'safe keeping' along with the convent seal and muniments) but also farm stock and household goods. They also had to take note of the names, ages, preferences between capacity and transfer, and moral reputation of each member of the community, and to catalogue all farmworkers and servants together with their rates of pay. The priory buildings, the church, cloister and domestic offices had also to be surveyed, described and evaluated, particular attention being paid to the amount of lead on the roofs and the number and weight of the bells. No detail was overlooked, and where the records of such 'supervisions' survive they provide a very comprehensive picture indeed of some of the lesser priories on the eve of their dissolution. Very different these were from the great abbeys with their lordly abbots, complex administration, far-flung estates and stately buildings which probably provide for most people their image of medieval monasticism, and for this reason it seems appropriate to append to this chapter a brief contemporary description of a typical small priory.

When the work of surveying and listing had been done at each house the commissioners would move on, leaving the brethren or nuns to continue their accustomed way of life until the king's further pleasure should be signified to them. Lest they should be tempted to allow the prospect of imminent dissolution to discourage them from caring for their property as they should, they were to be commanded by the commissioners to cultivate the land as hitherto, and warned that at a later date they would be called upon to account for all the possessions of their houses which had been technically the king's since the date of the passage of the dissolution act. Those who preserved the goods of their priories

'without spoil, waste, or embezzling the same'

would be most charitably dealt with when the time for dissolution came.

The Brief Certificates

At every house within their area the commissioners duly repeated this process of 'supervision'. They then prepared, and sent up to Augmentations, a 'brief certificate' or digest of the information which they had collected, and adjourned to await further instructions. Meanwhile the inhabitants of the supervised houses continued to pursue their accustomed routine, though the uncertainty of the future must have been very unsettling for them. With a few exceptions, where the commissioners had received special instructions to proceed to immediate dissolution, no house had been actually suppressed. And yet, deprived of the possession of their convent seals, their muniments, and their more valuable treasures, and obliged to keep a careful account of all consumption and expenditure, they were certainly no longer in control of their own affairs. Already some were engaged in negotiations which they hoped would lead to a grant of exemption. The earliest of such grants are dated 8 August 1536.

The surviving 'brief certificates' display some variation in form but clearly were all designed to serve the same purpose, to acquaint the officers of the court of Augmentations briefly with such information as would help them to decide how many houses would need to be spared in each district, and what ones they should be. The certificates, therefore, gave brief details for each house of its financial state, the total number of religious, corrodians, servants and other dependants living in it, the number who would accept capacities if the house should be suppressed, and some general comment upon the reputation of the religious persons dwelling there.

The sending in of the 'brief certificates' was followed in most areas by an interval of inactivity on the part of the suppression commissioners while the officers of Augmentations considered the information before them and made up their minds. Some of the factors they had to take into account we have already touched upon (see Chapter 5), but they were not left to make their decisions on the score of accommodation and numbers alone. From the very moment of the passing of the dissolution act letters from would-be purchasers of monastic lands had begun to pour in.

> '. . . if there be or shall be any such direction taken for abbeys that tempora men shall have any commodity thereby, I desire your mastership for my preferment in that behalf'

wrote Sir Henry Everington to Cromwell on 4 April 1536. Three days earlier Sir George Darcy had been much more specific about what he wanted

> '. . . I have written to the King's majesty to be good and gracious lord unto me as concerning the preferment of the nunnery of Swine abbey whereof my wife is foundress after the decease of her father . . .'.

Many others wrote in similar vein. Just occasionally the plea was that some particular house should be spared.

> '. . . the said prior and brethren are right well favoured and commended by the honest men of Hull and other neighbours thereabouts for their good living and great hospitality by them daily kept . . . and that it would please you . . . that they might continue in their said house . . .'

wrote the Yorkshire suppression commissioners on 28 May, two days after 'supervising' the Charterhouse in Hull. Sometimes there was also the hint of an offer of a bribe, but, taking all in all, the Augmentations officials, though they did grant exemption to Hull, do not seem to have paid very much attention to such outside pressures. Even the priors of Coxford and Horsham in Norfolk, to whom Cromwell wrote virtually promising exemption, did not in fact get it. On the other hand some properties which had been eagerly sought after, such as Swine, were left in the hands of the religious.

Suppressions and Exemptions

When the decisions had been made there followed another period of intense activity on the part of the suppression commissioners. Where a priory was to be allowed to stand, the convent seal, muniments and jewels had to be returned to the religious. Elsewhere the commissioners proceeded to dissolution. The prior or prioress was sent off to Augmentations to be pensioned. Of the remaining religious, those who had asked for capacities were sent to the archbishop or the Lord Chancellor who were empowered to make such grants. To help them on their way, and to defray the cost of purchasing the secular apparel appropriate to their new status, they were given on departure a gratuity, or 'reward', of something between twenty and thirty shillings, but that was all. Those who had asked to be allowed to remain in religion were duly dispatched to their new cloisters with letters of introduction and a small gratuity in their pockets. One or two who were too old or infirm to manage the journey were committed to the care of friendly neighbours and given a small allowance for their support.

The religious community was thus broken up, but the economic unity of the monastic estate was generally at first left undisturbed. Pending the making of some more permanent arrangement, the buildings of the priory and its demesne lands were usually committed to the care of some local man who was prepared to act as 'farmer', that is to rent them from the crown as they stood. Later, though not inevitably, the farmer might get a formal lease of the property, or even purchase it, but that was a matter for Augmentations to decide at leisure. The immediate concern of the suppression commissioners was to find someone to take over the property as a going concern.

The movable property of the house was disposed of in various ways. Anything of high intrinsic value, gold and silver plate, jewels, richly embroidered vestments or fine altar cloths, was gathered up by the commissioners and sent up to London, to the king's jewel house. Farmstock and household utensils were put up for sale on the spot, and were most frequently purchased by the farmer. The bells and roofing lead were, as valuable sources of metal, reserved for the king's use, and for the time being left in position.

The domestic staff was paid off, getting small gratuities in addition to any arrears of wages which might be owing to them. Their chances of re-employment cannot have been very good, for even if the new farmer should choose to reside on the property he would hardly need as large an establishment as had his predecessors. The farm workers received the same treatment as the domestics, but were frequently re-engaged by the new occupier. The treatment of corrodians and other dependants seems to have varied from house to house. Those who were able to show grants under convent seal fared best. Some, such as Elizabeth Ward at Moxby, seem to have accepted a single lump payment as compensation for the loss of all their rights and benefits. Others continued to receive from Augmentations annually for life the monetary equivalent of whatever benefits in kind they had formerly received. Those who had no formal grant to show the commissioners, but who depended entirely upon the informal charity of the religious fared worst. A small gratuity was the most that they could expect.

By the end of the summer of 1536 most of the work of the suppression commissioners had been done and the officials of the court of Augmentations had taken over the administration of the newly acquired properties. The monks and nuns at many of the houses which had been spared from suppression were now engaged in the lengthy and sometimes expensive process of getting formal confirmation of their exemption by letters patent under the great seal, as the dissolution act required. By no means all of them were successful in this. Of the sixty-seven houses exempted only fifty-one in the end obtained patents, and some of these had to wait a very long time for their grant. The series of grants of exemption starts on 8 August 1536 and continues to 13 May 1538. By this latter date the policy of partial dissolution had been abandoned in favour of that of total abolition, and it would have been pointless to have confirmed any more exemptions by formal grant.

Resistance

In most areas the work of dissolution proceeded smoothly enough. The religious accepted dispersal, their neighbours displayed no active sympathy. Indeed, to judge from the number of urgent applications which were made for the grant of particular monastic properties, the local gentry were more interested in the monks' estates than in the monks themselves, and were glad enough to see them go. In some parts of the country, however, the work of dissolution did not go off quite so smoothly.

G

Best known is the resistance put up by the Augustinian canons of Hexham in Northumberland. When the suppression commissioners arrived there late in the season, towards the end of September, they found the gates of the priory closed and the canons prepared to resist by force any attempt to evict them. They claimed further to have a grant of exemption from suppression under the great seal which they eventually showed to the commissioners who were genuinely perplexed by this document which was so patently in conflict with their own instructions. Their perplexity was for the time being resolved by the outbreak of the great northern rising which secured for the canons of Hexham a respite until 26 February 1537. Then, with the restoration of royal authority in the north, their house was quietly suppressed. No further resistance was offered, but on the other hand the canons do not appear to have been penalised in any way for their earlier opposition to suppression.

Another Augustinian house, that of Norton in Cheshire, was also the scene of an attempt to resist suppression. There the commissioners had actually taken possession of the abbey and dismissed the monks when the abbot returned at the head of a sizeable armed band and besieged the commissioners in a tower. The siege, however, was a short one. The arrival that same night of a more efficient force of loyal subjects under the command of the sheriff scattered the besiegers, relieved the commissioners, and secured the arrest of the abbot and a few of his collaborators.

At Sawley, on the borders of Yorkshire and Lancashire, the Cistercian monks did not actively resist the suppression of their house in May, or its transfer to Sir Arthur Darcy who purchased the household and farm stock and entered into immediate possession, but it is clear from their subsequent actions that they were exceedingly reluctant to accept the change as irreversible. Only four of the twenty-one monks there did not obtain capacities, but expressed a wish to remain in religion. After the suppression of their house these four went to Furness to join the community there. The abbot of Furness later claimed that they had also had capacities, and had had, therefore, no right to lodging in his abbey. Consequently he had refused to admit them, and they had returned to the neighbourhood of their former home. What the other monks did we cannot say for certain, but it is clear that none of them went very far afield, for when the great northern rising began in October 1536, five months after their eviction from their convent, they were all near at hand and ready and willing to re-enter the cloister and resume their former way of life. Indeed Sir Arthur Darcy was quite sure that it was the monks themselves who had taken the initiative and 'stirred and procured' the rebellion in order to secure their own return. The abbot tried to exculpate himself and to put the blame on the local people, but the fact that the whole community was so promptly restored at the very beginning of the rebellion does suggest strongly that they had been at the very least holding themselves in readiness for such an event, if not actively preparing for it.

But these examples of resistance to suppression are exceptional. As a rule the majority of the religious accepted their fate with good grace, or with quiet resignation.

APPENDIX: A CONTEMPORARY ACCOUNT OF A SMALL NUNNERY

Extracts from the Suppression Commissioners' Papers relating to the Cistercian priory of Handale in Yorkshire.

(All these extracts derive originally from one source, the second volume of the MS Suppression Papers in the Public Record Office. Most of the contents of this particular volume, which is composed entirely of a most heterogeneous collection of the actual working papers of the suppression commissioners with all their alterations, erasures, insertions and marginal notes, has been printed, the descriptions of priory buildings in vol. IX of the *Yorkshire Archaeological Journal*, the greater part of the remainder in vol. LXXX of the *Yorkshire Archaeological Society's Record Series*. Extracts nos. 1, 3 & 4 have been taken, with spelling modernised, from the printed versions. Extract no. 2, in which an attempt is made to produce the original reading of a twice-used and much altered list, comes, with abbreviations extended, direct from the MS)

1. THE PRIORY BUILDINGS
Handale, Scitus Domorum

The church containeth in length 60 foot and in breadth 16 foot, with a low roof covered with lead, having 7 glass windows containing 50 foot of glass by estimation, with a high altar, 2 altars in the choir and one beneath the choir.

Item the cloister at the south side of the church containeth in length 48 foot square and 5 foot broad, one quarter of it covered with lead having no glass.

Note that the dorter and chambers are over 3 parts of the same cloister.

Item the dorter at the east part of the church containeth in length 48 foot and in breadth 16 foot, timber walls within and stone walls without, with a low roof and covered with lead.

Item there is the chapter house and one little chamber and an old chamber under the said dorter.

Item 3 low chambers at the south part of the cloister whereof one is the larder house.

Item the garner over the said chambers at the south part of the cloister containing 40 foot long and 16 foot broad, stone walls, a low roof, and covered with lead.

Item a guest chamber at the nether end of the said garner and over the cloister, containing 16 foot square with a chimney and covered with lead, having two windows part glazed containing 5 foot of glass.

Item another chamber by the same containing 20 foot long and 12 foot broad, stone walls, a chimney, and covered with (*blank*)

Item the high hall over the west part of the cloister, containing 24 foot long and 20 foot broad, stone walls, a chimney, 4 little windows part glazed containing 10 foot of glass, and a low roof covered with lead.

Item the parlour by the same containing in length 20 foot and in breadth 12 foot, with a chimney, stone walls, a low roof and covered with lead.

Item at the west part of the cloister under the hall a little chamber with a chimney, a buttery, and another little chamber by the same.

Item the kitchen at the nether end of the hall, containing 16 foot square with a chimney of stone, and covered with lead.

Item a little parlour by the said kitchen containing 12 foot square with a chimney and . . .

Item the brewhouse and boulting house containing in length 40 foot and in breadth 18 foot whereof 18 foot covered with slates and 22 foot with thatch, daubed walls, somewhat out of reparation.

Item an old house having a hall and one low chamber and 2 little chambers above, containing in length 36 foot and in breadth 18 foot, old stone walls, covered with thatch, decayed.

Item 2 chambers over the gates going into the inner court containing 30 foot long and 16 foot broad, timber walls white-limed and well covered with slates.

Item 2 low chambers under the same 2.

Item an old house where they lay turf or fuel containing 30 foot long and 14 foot broad with old mud walls covered with thatch, decayed.

Item one stable at the end of the brewhouse containing 14 foot long and 10 foot broad, daubed walls and covered with thatch.

Item the kiln house containing 40 foot long and 14 foot broad, daubed walls and covered with thatch.

Item the cow house 40 foot long and 16 foot broad, with old walls much broken and ill covered with thatch, decayed.

Item a barn a little from the house, containing 60 foot long and 24 foot broad, timber walls and well covered with thatch.

Item the ox house by the barn containing 50 foot long and 16 foot broad, daubed walls and covered with thatch.

Item a calf house 30 foot long and 14 foot broad, covered with thatch.

Item there is a little overshot mill going with a little water, daubed walls and covered with thatch.

2. The Nuns

Note that they all be of good living

	Anna Lutton prioress	aged 48 years	
	Johanna Scot	aged 90 years, blind.	Note that
Religion	Alice Brampton	aged 70 years	this woman
Religion	Agnes Peghan	aged 62 years	is blind
Religion	Margaret Loghan	aged 42 years	
Religion	Isabella Norman	aged 26 years	
Religion	Cicilia Watson	aged 28 years	
8 Religion	Anna Denyson	aged 24 years	

3. The Servants

Servants' wages paid and rewards given to them.

First given in reward to Agnes Loghan, having a corrody there, 5/.

Item given to an old gentlewoman named Elizabeth Bryan, in reward 6/8.

Item to John Sawyer chief husband servant for his quarter wages at Lammas 4/3 and in reward 2/5.   6/8.

Item to John Coverdale miller for like wages at Lammas 2/9 and in reward 2/3.   5/-.

Item to Gilbert Benyson boy for his quarter wages 2/- and reward 20*d*.   3/8.

Item to Matthew Carlill a boy for like   3/8.

Item to Mary Lutton butler for her quarter wages at Lammas 21*d*. and in reward 3/3.   5/-.

Item to Margaret Hodshon cook for her quarter wages 2/3 and reward 2/9.   5/-.

Item to Elizabeth Carlill for her quarter wages 21*d*. and reward 3/3.   5/-.

Item to Cristabel Boyes for her quarter wages 15*d*. and reward 2/1.   3/4.

Item to Thomas Henryson chaplain for his quarter wages 10/– and reward 3/4.   13/4.

                                                  62/4.

4. A CORRODY

The corrody of Richard Loghan and Agnes Loghan

First a house to dwell in yearly,	Nil, because it remains there.
Item 7 loaves of bread weekly, weighing every loaf 2 pounds,	26/–
Item 6 gallons of convent ale and 1 gallon small ale weekly,	26/–
Item half a cow yearly,	5/–
Item a whole swine yearly,	20*d*.
Item a bushel oats,	12*d*.
Item a bushel peas,	4*d*.
Item a bushel and a half salt yearly,	8*d*.
Item 7 salt fishes yearly,	14*d*.
Item 100 herrings white and red,	10*d*.
Item of every mutton that were killed 1*d*.	4/4
Item of every beast that were killed,	6*d*.
4 loads turves yearly,	20*d*.
A load wood,	6*d*.
Milk of a cow winter and summer,	2/–
Item from Easter to Martinmas every week a quart milk,	8*d*.
Item every principal feast to dine with the prioress and convent,	8*d*.
Every year 1 lb. candles,	1*d*.

Sum Total 73/1.

7

The Pilgrimage of Grace

THROUGHOUT the spring and summer of 1536 the suppression commissioners were hard at work in every part of the country, and by September the greater part of their work was done. In early October of the same year there began the great protest in arms which we call the Pilgrimage of Grace. This rebellion followed so closely upon the suppression of the lesser monasteries that it is clearly impossible to suppose that there was no connection between the two events. Nevertheless it must always be remembered that this great northern rising was a many sided affair, and not simply a protest against the dissolution of the smaller religious houses. The pilgrims' own list of six major grievances is headed, it is true, by the 'Suppression of the Religious Houses', but it embraces also the Act of Uses, the Act of First Fruits, the lay subsidy, the base-born councillors about the king, and the newly appointed bishops, some of whom were suspected of heretical tendencies. In addition to these publicly expressed grievances some of the rebels were also spurred to action by resentment against the increasing interference of the government in economic affairs, by personal hardships resulting from the contemporary inflation, and by the age-old jealousy between South and North.

The Rebels and the Religious

The dissolution of the lesser abbeys was not the 'cause' of the Pilgrimage of Grace in the sense that without it there would have been no rebellion. At the most it was the proverbial 'last straw' which also provided the rebels with a popular cause and a good rallying cry in the 'preservation of Christ's Church'. The action of the suppression commissioners in gathering up and carrying off so many rich treasures which had graced the religious houses for so many years would have brought home to the villagers and countryfolk far more effectively than any pronouncements of convocation or parliament about the headship of the church the fact that great changes were on foot, that the church as they had known it all their lives was in danger of overthrow by the base-born councillors and heretically-inclined bishops who had gained control of king and government. 'Crim, Crame and Riche' were the three evil geniuses singled out for specific mention in the pilgrims' marching hymn. 'Crim' was Cromwell, the base-born councillor. 'Crame' was Cranmer, the chief of the heretical bishops. 'Riche' was Sir Richard Rich, first chancellor of the court of Augmentations, and in that capacity chiefly responsible for the administration of the dissolution.

Even if we are not prepared to believe that many of the suppressors were as careless of local sentiment as those who are alleged to have used rich copes and ornate vestments from monastic churches as saddle-cloths for their horses, we can still appreciate the extent of the shock that must have been experienced by many who witnessed this sudden spoiling of ancient priories. Indeed, one of the rumours which helped to precipitate the rising in Lincolnshire was the widely believed story that after the monasteries the parish churches were next on the list for plundering.

The dissolution of the lesser abbeys therefore helped to give effective shape to a mixed body of grievances of many kinds and to provide rebels of diverse classes and interests with a popular common cause. But how wholeheartedly did the religious orders, on whose behalf the rebels so consistently claimed to be acting, support the movement or commit themselves to the pilgrim cause?

To answer this question we must first distinguish between the monks and nuns from some of the smaller houses who had already suffered eviction from their cloisters by virtue of the dissolution act, and those in the larger and exempted abbeys who were still in possession and had hitherto been permitted to continue their accustomed way of life with very little interruption. Of the former group quite a number seem to have taken advantage of the rising and returned to their former homes. The evidence for such returns is, in some cases, very slight, but taken all in all, is just about sufficient to support the view that a substantial proportion of the evicted religious returned to their cloisters. It is not possible, however, to say categorically that they all went back.

The Restoration of the Dispossessed

It is quite clear that the restoration of the evicted religious was part of the rebels' programme. At an early stage in the rising the pilgrim leader, Robert Aske, issued orders designed to regulate such restorations and the conduct of the monks and nuns after their return. It would appear from these orders that the rebel leaders had no desire to defy statute or to ignore the authority of parliament. Their view seems to have been that the king and his parliament had been misled into giving their approval to the policy of suppression, and that, once the earnest desire of the common people of the northern regions that the dissolved houses should be restored was made plain, the next parliament, to be held, it was hoped, in York, would readily assent to a repeal of the dissolution act. Meanwhile, in anticipation of such a repeal, the unjustly dispossessed religious should once again enjoy possession of the properties to which they would soon be legally restored. At the same time, however, the rights and interest of the new lay possessors had also to be protected, and Aske's orders took care to see that they were. Though the lay occupiers (the 'king's farmers') were required by the rebels to readmit the former monks and nuns and to supply them with all the necessities of life, a careful record was to be kept, by indenture between the farmer and the religious, of all that was thus supplied, presumably so that at some later date the farmers could receive appropriate compensation for their losses. If the farmers were willing to co-operate in this scheme they were to be left technically 'in possession' of the property of their houses, if not, they were to be evicted and the religious restored to full possession. But even then the monks were required by Aske to keep an account of all the goods that they consumed pending the ultimate settlement of the whole question. Any attempt to despoil the farmers was to be punishable by death. As the suppression act had endeavoured to protect the legitimate interests of all parties, even so this pilgrim order for the restoration of the religious attempted to protect the newly acquired interests of the recently instituted farmers who had, in the majority of cases, given good money for their farmstock and household goods, and were in no sense expropriators themselves.

On these terms quite a number of the evicted religious returned to their convents. The exact number who did so cannot now be ascertained, nor can we be sure that the oft-quoted, but unspecific, account of the general rejoicing which followed the issue of Aske's orders refers to any but the religious houses in York city itself. According to this account the people were so delighted with the order for restoration that they then and there insisted upon escorting the religious back to their cloisters in a cheering torchlight procession.

In the counties chiefly affected by the rising, Lincolnshire, Yorkshire, Durham, Northumberland, Cumberland, Westmorland and Lancashire, some seventy-five small priories had been selected for suppression under the terms of the 1536 act. In Lincolnshire, not one of the twenty affected seems to have been restored, though some of the suppression commissioners fell into the rebels' hands. In the other six counties there is evidence of one sort or another to confirm the restoration of the monks and nuns of sixteen of the fifty-five suppressed priories. The best documented case of restoration is that of the Cistercian abbey of Sawley on the Ribble.

The Monks of Sawley

At Sawley, as we have already noticed (see Chapter 6), the abbot and all his monks were ready at hand to re-enter their abbey at the very beginning of the rebellion. Having evicted the representatives of the new lay owner, Sir Arthur Darcy, on 12 October 1536, they resumed the normal pattern of claustral life. Their house became at once the centre of disaffection of the borders of Yorkshire and Lancashire, and they seem to have lent the rebels their wholehearted support. One of the monks is generally credited with the authorship of the pilgrims' marching song which begins:

> 'Christ crucified
> For thy wounds wide
> Us Commons guide
>   Which pilgrims be
> Through God's grace
> For to purchase
> Old wealth and peace
>   Of the spiritualty.'

Another, perhaps the abbot himself, made an interesting excursion into political theory when he composed, and in all likelihood preached, a sermon declaring the lawfulness of taking up arms in defence of the faith.

By their enthusiasm for the rebel cause the monks of Sawley attracted to themselves the particular displeasure of the king who instructed the earl of Derby (in command of the loyal forces of south Lancashire and Cheshire) to advance upon the abbey and, if he found any of the monks there, to hang them in their habits as 'most arrant traitors and movers of insurrection'.[1] But, before the earl had any opportunity to test his arms against the rebels, the royal commander in Yorkshire, the duke of Norfolk, had on 27 October agreed to a general truce, and Derby was instructed to dismiss his men.

And so the monks of Sawley were for the time being spared, and continued to enjoy possession of their house and cloister for nearly four months more. Then, in February 1537, the outbreak of a second and more localised rising in the East Riding of Yorkshire gave the king the excuse he needed for breaking the truce, and the duke of Norfolk was sent north once again to crush the now divided rebels. Once again the monks of Sawley were singled out for special mention, though this time, in the king's instructions to Norfolk, they were bracketed with all others who had

'in any wise conspired or kept their houses with any force'.

All such were to be dealt with 'without pity or circumstance' and were to be

'tied up without further delay or ceremony, to the terrible example of others'.

In the end the abbot was captured, tried, probably on a charge of treason, and condemned. There is, however, no record of his exection, but neither is there any evidence that he survived. As he had been reported 'sore diseased and not like long to continue' in 1536, it may well be that death saved him from the executioner. Of his monks, one, his chaplain, was hanged at nearby Whalley, and two others were excepted from the general pardon, but seem to have made good their escape. The fate of the remaining eighteen is not known. Their names simply disappear from the record.

The king's letter to the duke of Norfolk, ordering the summary execution of all who, like the monks of Sawley, had 'kept their

[1] For the full text of this famous letter, see the appendix to this chapter.

houses with any force', mentions four other convents by name, Hexham and Newminster in Northumberland, Lanercost in Cumberland, and St. Agatha's near Richmond. The first of these, as we have seen (see chapter 6), had not in fact been dissolved when the rising broke out. About the others we know little more than this letter tells us. None of the four was treated as severely as Sawley. Even the canons of Hexham do not appear to have suffered for their resistance to suppression before the rising.

Besides these five, there is evidence to confirm that the nuns of Clementhorpe, just outside the walls of York, and those from Nunburnholme in the East Riding, also returned to their convents during the rebellion, as did some at least of the monks of Holy Trinity priory in York city. In Lancashire the monks of Cartmel and Conishead were restored, though the prior of the former house fled to the royal host. It is also clear that at Newcastle some of the Observant Franciscans, whose whole order had been suppressed for refusing the oath to the succession in 1534, were also for a short time restored, as were some of the canons from Coverham, Ferriby and Haltemprice. In a few more instances there are references in the Augmentation office accounts which suggest, but do not directly testify to, the return of religious persons to their cloisters during the disturbances. For the remainder of the suppressed northern priories, however, there is no evidence one way or the other, and we are left to put our own construction upon the silence of the record.

As such information as we do possess about the return of evicted monks and nuns to their houses during the Pilgrimage of Grace is so fragmentary it is far from easy to decide just who was chiefly responsible for their restoration. After the suppression of the rising all concerned were anxious to deny having taken the initiative in what might well be held to be a treasonable act. The abbot of Sawley blamed the common people of the district, and claimed that it was against his will that he and his brethren had been restored to their abbey. The prior of Cartmel showed by his desertion to the royal side that he too had been an unwilling participant in the restoration of his brethren. William Hungate, farmer of Nunburnholme, also attributed responsibility to the local inhabitants, led in this instance by the rector of the parish. At Clementhorpe it was said that 'those knaves which now be up in Yorkshire' were to blame for the restoration of the nuns.

On the other hand Sir Arthur Darcy, lay owner of Sawley, preferred, as we have seen (see chapter 6), to lay the principal blame upon the religious themselves, and this much can be said in support of his point of view, that whoever first suggested that the dispossessed monks and nuns should re-enter their convents, the latter certainly showed little reluctance to act upon the suggestion once it was made. They none of them seem to have strayed very far from their former homes, nor do they appear to have been at all hesitant accomplices in the rebellion, once it had begun.

The Involvement of the Greater Abbeys

Rather different was the attitude towards the rebellion of the inhabitants of the larger abbeys which the suppression act had left untouched. They were far from enthusiastic about the pilgrim cause, but their position was admittedly a very difficult one. They had little to gain, and all to lose, by association with rebellion. There was nothing as yet in the activities of the government or its agents to suggest that it was intended to abolish monasticism altogether. Indeed, as we have seen, the indications so far had been all the other way, to the effect that the partial dissolution resulting from the statute of 1536 was all that the authorities had in mind. And, as we shall see, the way in which those larger abbeys which did get involved in the Pilgrimage of Grace were dealt with would seem to indicate that even after the suppression of the rebellion there was still no intention of proceeding to total dissolution. A rising which included in its aims the restoration of the lesser abbeys would, if successful, bring no immediate advantage to the larger houses and, if unsuccessful, would involve all who participated in it in the meshes of the treason laws. And yet the rebels from the very beginning made it perfectly clear that they thought that, as they were rising on behalf of the dispossessed religious, those still in possession were morally bound to offer them every assistance.

In Lincolnshire when the rebels turned to the abbeys of Kirkstead and Barlings for support, they found that they had to threaten to burn down the two houses before the monks could be persuaded to co-operate in a satisfactory manner. In Yorkshire the experience of the pilgrims was generally similar. Sir Nicholas Fairfax, one of the leaders there, thought that

'as it was a spiritual matter all churchmen should go forth in person' and dispatched George Lumley on a tour of the major monastic establishments of the shire to call on the abbots and priors to come to the pilgrim musters with their processional crosses and two of their brethren to attend them. Lumley was also to solicit contributions to the campaign fund.

Some abbots, including those of Byland and Whitby and the prior of Bridlington, duly sent subscriptions. One or two, including, surprisingly enough, the abbot of Rievaulx who had owed his election only three years earlier to Cromwell's patronage (see chapter 4), offered to come in person, but Aske overrode Fairfax and forbade them. The abbot of St. Mary's in York was not so easily excused attendance in person. When the pilgrims marched through that city they insisted upon his walking at the head of their procession bearing the abbey's finest cross. Reluctantly the abbot complied, but at the earliest opportunity slipped away, leaving his cross in pilgrim hands. The abbot of Kirkstall seems to have been a rather more enthusiastic pilgrim. He and his chaplain attended the rebel 'convocation' at Pontefract in December 1536, and in the following month he took advantage of the general disorder to pay off some old score by 'making a fray' against some of the servants of Sir Christopher Danby.

Abbot Sedbar of Jervaulx

One of the greater northern abbeys which became deeply implicated in the rising was the Cistercian house of Jervaulx whose abbot, Adam Sedbar, was to be executed as a consequence of his involvement. Sedbar's story is in many ways typical, and vividly illustrates the difficulties of the situation into which he and some of his fellow abbots were driven by the rising.

The monks of Jervaulx found themselves caught up in the insurrection on two distinct occasions. The first was on 11 October 1536, in the earliest days of the rebellion, when a band of insurgents descended upon the abbey and called for the abbot to come forth. Sedbar, however, had fled for refuge to nearby Witton fell, and there he lay low for four whole days, returning to the abbey only at night. His reluctance to lend support to the pilgrim cause is also indicated by his threat to dismiss on the spot any abbey servant who should choose to join the rebel band. The rebels were not, however, to be quite so easily discouraged, and were determined to secure the abbot's support. And so, on Sunday, 15 October, when Sedbar still failed to appear, they ordered the monks to consider their abbot deposed and to elect a successor, threatening that they would burn down the abbey if their order were not obeyed.

Obediently the monks rang the chapter bell and assembled to consider what action they should take. Objections against the holding of a new election being too strong to be set aside, a search party was sent out which located the abbot in his refuge and persuaded him to come back to the abbey to save it from the threatened destruction. On his return Sedbar was at first roughly handled by the rebels and threatened with immediate execution, but eventually milder counsels prevailed and the pilgrims contented themselves with compelling him to take their oath and to go with two of his brethren to the great rebel muster which was to be held at Darlington the next day.

When he saw there how formidable a host the rebels had gathered, and how widely their cause was supported, Sedbar seems to have shed some of his initial reluctance, for he was reported as saying openly that the rebel cause was so good that men would serve it for less than half the money which had been promised to men in the king's service. After a couple of days with the pilgrim host the abbot of Jervaulx was allowed to return home. Though his abbey was used by the rebels as a communications centre for a further week, Sedbar does not seem to have played any further part in the first rising.

The second occasion upon which the abbot and monks of Jervaulx became involved in rebellion was in February 1537 when two local agitators tried once more to raise the commons, and called upon the monks for aid. Remembering the perilous days of October Sedbar was this time more co-operative. He set meat and drink before the rebel leaders and asked them, with a show of deference, to excuse him and his brethren from joining the rebel host that day. They could take his servants if they wished. He and his brethren would join them the following day. Satisfied with these fair words the unwelcome visitors withdrew, whereupon the abbot fled to the security of Bolton castle where he remained until all danger was past. The rebels failed to receive the support which they had anticipated, and the rising collapsed of its own accord.

Executions and Forfeitures

For his very small part in this second, and very minor, disturbance, Sedbar was tried for treason and condemned to death. His exploits in the previous October were not held against him, for they had been covered by the general pardon granted to the rebels on 8 December 1536 and covering all acts committed up to that date. His actions since the pardon were scarcely treasonable, and in any case the rebels' threats could be pleaded in extenuation, but any such plea was brushed aside, for the government had discovered a new and convenient legal doctrine which held that the condemnation of an abbot for treason should result in the forfeiture to the crown of all the property of the abbey, just as if it were a lay fief in the personal possession of the abbot. Sedbar's condemnation was a foregone conclusion. His fault lay more in his office than in his acts. Three days before his trial began, and four days before his final condemnation, the king had already written to the duke of Norfolk and ordered him to proceed to the dissolution of Sedbar's abbey.

Of course Adam Sedbar was not the only abbot to be executed for alleged treasons committed during the course of the rising. Indeed the doctrine of forfeiture was first applied to the Lancashire Cistercian house of Whalley whose abbot, John Paslew, was executed on 10 March 1537 for, among other things, having harboured one of the rebellious monks from nearby Sawley. The abbots of Kirkstead and Barlings and the prior of Bridlington, though they, like Sedbar, had only joined the rebels under duress and had extricated themselves at the earliest opportunity, were likewise condemned to die and their houses forfeit. Several lesser religious persons, including four canons from Cartmel, six monks from Bardney, one from Louth Park, and the former abbot of Fountains who was resident at Jervaulx at the time of the second rising, were also executed, but as they were not governors of houses their deaths did not involve any further forfeitures.

There was, however, no wholesale massacre of monks or nuns. Those who had returned to the suppressed houses were, with the exceptions already noted, allowed to go in peace. The former heads of Clementhorpe, Nunburnholme and Holy Trinity York were duly paid their pensions in 1538 and subsequent years, and the clemency thus shown to the heads was almost certainly extended to the other members as well. The monks of Whalley, with the exception of one who suffered execution alongside his abbot, were dismissed with gratuities of 40s. each and the choice between capacities or transfer to other houses of their order. The pattern established there was prob-

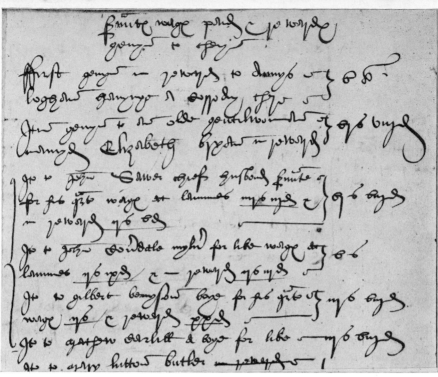

5 The Servants at Handale: the first part of the list which is given in full in the appendix to Chapter 6

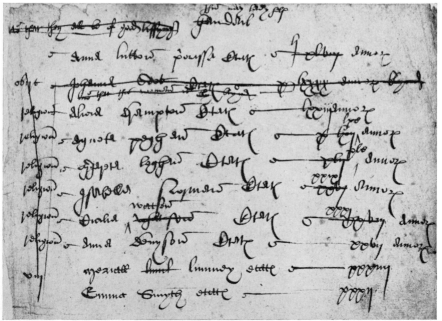

6 The Nuns of Handale: a list first drawn up in 1536 and revised in 1539. A reading of the first version is given in the appendix to Chapter 6

7 Kirkstall: view from the south-west. A well preserved church and cloister of the normal Cistercian plan

8 Jervaulx: view from the north-west. The foundations of the church can be traced in the left foreground. To the east of the clearly marked cloister can be seen the outlines of the chapter house with the slender columns which once supported the ceiling. South of this is a portion of the dorter wall, behind which lie the remains of the abbot's lodging and the infirmary ably followed at Bridlington, Barlings and Kirkstead too, and this continued use of the procedure of transfer as provided for in the dissolution act of 1536 shows quite clearly that as yet there was no thought in the government's mind of making an end of the abbeys altogether.

Precedents for Surrender

And yet the treatment meted out to one abbey, Furness, foreshadowed the future. At that large Cistercian house in north Lancashire some of the monks had openly expressed their sympathy with the rebel cause, but it was not easy to find any plausible excuse for charging the abbot with treason and so securing the forfeiture of the abbey. However, the abbot was very ready to oblige and responded with alacrity to an almost casual suggestion that he might make a voluntary surrender of his abbey and its property into the hands of the crown. And thus was another precedent set, and one which was to be even more useful to the government in years to come than the precedent of Whalley. What was implicit in the surrender of Furness was the doctrine that the abbot and monks for the time being had the power by their own action to terminate the existence of a perpetual corporation of which they were at the best life trustees. Almost all the greater abbeys were eventually to come into the hands of the crown as a consequence of similar acts of surrender. There were to be no further acts of suppression. The act of 1539 (31 Henry VIII c. 13) which is sometimes called 'the second dissolution act', did not transfer to the crown the property of a single abbey. Its sole purpose was to set at rest the doubts which seem to have arisen in some minds about the validity of deeds of surrender, to legalise retroactively such surrenders as had taken place, and prospectively all that might yet occur.

And so the Pilgrimage of Grace, which from its very beginning had had the restoration of the dispossessed religious as one of its objects, was only reluctantly and under pressure supported by the monks of the larger abbeys, and resulted in the establishment of important precedents for surrender and forfeiture which were to be of considerable assistance to the government once it was decided to make an end of the religious orders altogether.

H

APPENDIX:
THE EARL OF DERBY'S INSTRUCTIONS

(From *The Correspondence of Edward, Third Earl of Derby*, edited for the Chetham Society by T. N. Toller, 1890. Upon the outbreak of the Pilgrimage of Grace the earl of Derby was commissioned to raise forces for the suppression of the rising in his own area, south Lancashire. He was, however, subordinate in command to the earl of Shrewsbury and the duke of Norfolk, in succession royal commanders in the main theatre, south Yorkshire. Given below, with the spelling modernised, are the commission empowering Derby to raise troops and the letter instructing him to deal mercilessly with the monks of Sawley. Derby was on the point of marching from Preston towards Sawley when he was stopped by a letter from Shrewsbury sending him news of the truce made at Doncaster on 27 October and instructing him to disband his forces.)

The King's Commission sent to my Lord

Henry, by the grace of God King of England and of France, defender of the faith, Lord of Ireland and in earth supreme head of the Church of England; to our right trusty and right well beloved Cousin, the earl of Derby, greeting. Forasmuch as we be credibly informed that divers seditious persons in the parts of Lancashire and thereabouts have lately assembled themselves most traitorously together, and so rebelliously attempted divers things contrary to their duties of allegiance to us their Prince and Sovereign Lord, our pleasure and commandment is that, by virtue of this our Commission, you shall levy our people and force in the parts of Lancashire and thereabouts above said, and with the same address yourself speedily to all such places where any such rebellion hath been attempted, and there either to cause them to submit themselves for their offences to our grace and mercy and likewise to declare unto you the setters on of their insurrection, or else to subdue them with such force, extremity and violence as all other by their example may beware of like attempts. And therefore we will and most straitly charge and command all Mayors, Sheriffs, Bailiffs, Constables and all other our Officers, Ministers, Subjects and true liegemen, of what estate, condition or degree soever they be, inhabiting within our said County of Lancaster or upon the borders of the same, not only to go with you with all their forces and in all things follow your direction and appointment in the premises, but also from place to place to see you and your company for your reasonable money furnished with victuals, carriage and all other things convenient for your conveyance or demur, as you shall limit and appoint them, without failing, as they will show themselves our true and faithful subjects, and for the contrary answer at their perils. Given under our privy seal, the 20th day of October, the 28th year of our reign.

The third letter sent to my Lord by the King with this foresaid Commission.

Right trusty and right well beloved Cousin, we greet you well. And whereas by our former letters addressed unto you we gave you specially in commandment not only to put your forces in readiness, but also upon advertisement from our Cousin of Shrewsbury, our Lieutenant for the repression of the rebellion in the north parts, with all your said forces speedily to address yourself unto him, wheresoever he should chance to be; understanding since then that there hath been like insurrection and assembly lately attempted in the borders of Lancashire, specially about the abbey of Sawley and other parts thereabout, insomuch the abbot and monks be again by the traitors of that assembly restored to the possession of the said abbey, as we be informed: we have determined and resolved, anything in our said former letters to the contrary hereof notwithstanding, to command you that, gathering all your forces together and calling unto you all the gentlemen of the country thereabouts, you shall immediately upon the sight hereof proceed with the same to the repression of the said rebellion and assembly in the said borders of Lancashire or elsewhere within or near the same, if any such do yet continue. And so semblably to the repression of all such like attempts that shall be enterprised in those parts, and to travail to the uttermost of your power to apprehend the captains and chief doers of the same and incontinently to cause them like traitors to be executed there; specially in your own person with all your said forces to the said abbey of Sawley, in case there be not more need of redress in other places; in which case ye shall address first that which hath most need and after do the other. And if ye shall find the late abbot and monks thereof remaining in the possession of the house, having received it again at the hands of such traitors and rebels, we will then ye shall take the said abbot and monks with their assistants forth with violence and without any manner of delay, in their monks' apparel, cause them to be hanged up as most arrant traitors and movers of insurrection and sedition accordingly; having special regard and especial care throughout all the country and parts about you that no town or village begin once to assemble or gather together but that they may immediately with the sword be repressed to the terrible example of all others in time coming. And this matter for your parts round about you we desire and pray you like a man of your honour to attend, and in no wise to depart to our said Cousin of Shrewsbury as we before appointed. And doubt you not we shall so remember your charges and consider your service that you shall have cause to be satisfied and contented. And for your sufficient authority for the purpose to levy our forces and people in those parts about you we send unto you herewith a commission under our privy signet at our castle of Windsor the 20th day of October, the 28th year of our reign.

8

Suppression by Surrender

THE suppression of the Pilgrimage of Grace was not followed by any immediate change in the policy of the government towards the religious orders. The property of the forfeited abbeys, and that of Furness, was taken into the hands of the crown and disposed of at a leisurely pace.

The Forfeited Abbeys

In the last week of May 1537 the duke of Norfolk was at Jervaulx, supervising the dispatch of the religious and the disposal of the household goods and furnishings. Much of the latter was, at the duke's suggestion, sent to Sheriff Hutton castle which was being prepared as headquarters for the newly created Council of the North. The more substantial assets of the abbey were more carefully handled. It seems likely that the full value of some of the smaller priories dissolved in the previous year had not been realised for the crown because of the speed with which their lands had been leased or sold. Sir Arthur Darcy, for instance

'never knew what Sawley was till it was granted'

for he received his lands 'unsurveyed'. Greater care was therefore taken now with the lands of the forfeited abbeys, and no leases were granted until a full and careful survey had been made. This process was not completed at Jervaulx until the beginning of August, and at Barlings and Kirkstead not until even later. Even then there was no rush to admit tenants. The first formal lease of lands formerly belonging to Jervaulx is dated January 1538.

The movable assets of the forfeited houses were more speedily dealt with. Jewels and plate were, as before, reserved to the crown, and those from Bridlington and Jervaulx were sent up to London in June. The roofing lead, of which there was an abundance (that at Kirkstead and Jervaulx being worth, in the surveyor's estimation, at least £1,000, and that at Bridlington only a little less) was, after some delay occasioned by the inefficiency of the refiner, taken down, melted and carted away over roads

'so foul and steep that no carriage can pass in winter'.

The abbey bells were offered for sale locally, but did not command a good enough price and so were also sent up to the capital. By the autumn of 1537 the work of suppressing the forfeited houses was almost complete.

In the meantime no further suppressions had taken place. The monks and nuns whom the rebels had restored to their convents were evicted once more and their properties returned to the lay proprietors, but the houses which had been exempted from the force of the suppression statute continued to enjoy that exemption whether or not it was confirmed by letters patent. There is no evidence to suggest that any of the large number of small northern priories which enjoyed exemption from suppression under the act owed that exemption to the pilgrims' actions. Only exceptionally, in such instances as that of Hexham, had the work of the suppression commissioners been temporarily interrupted by the rising, and in every case the restoration of order had been followed immediately by the dissolution of the house in question. No other exempted house was touched until July 1538, and only a few before September of that year, by which time the suppression of the larger abbeys was well under way.

Thus, during the greater part of the year 1537 there was no outward indication of any intention on the part of the government to press forward its attack upon the religious orders, or to advance beyond the policy of partial dissolution and rational reorganisation implicit in the statute of 1536. A few monasteries whose abbots had been involved in rebellion had been forfeited to the crown, and one had surrendered without waiting for formal charges to be made, but there was as yet no sign that the remaining religious houses, which still numbered well over 500 when friaries, cells, Gilbertine houses and small exempted priories are all counted up, were in any danger. Monasticism still had strong roots in England, and the religious orders were still a familiar and accepted part of everyday life.

The Change in Policy

The first indications of a change in government policy began to appear in the last weeks of 1537. We cannot now say for certain when the decision to make a clean sweep of all the abbeys was taken, or if, indeed, such a decision was ever consciously taken at all. It may be that from the very first Cromwell and his associates were feeling their way, testing how far they could go without arousing serious opposition, and that we should not, for that reason, make too much of what was no more than a change in their method of proceeding. And yet, as we have already seen (see Chapter 5), there were certain provisions incorporated in the dissolution statute of 1536 which strongly suggested that total dissolution was not at that time contemplated, while in late 1537 and early 1538 there began to appear signs which equally strongly suggest that total dissolution was by then the accepted ultimate aim.

In the first place, in November 1537 the process of dissolution began again. The year 1536 had seen the smaller abbeys suppressed by statute. The spring of 1537 had witnessed the seizure and forfeiture of a few of the larger houses. Then, on 11 November, some seven months after the surrender of Furness, the precedent there set was repeated at Lewes in Sussex. The prior of this great and wealthy house had been in some danger of a charge of treason at the time of the general visitation in 1535 and, perhaps, his former indiscretions were now used to put pressure on him to persuade his brethren to join with him in resigning their house into the king's hands. Doubtless too the alternatives were made quite clear to the monks. Either they resigned now and received adequate compensation or they ran the risk of an indictment and all that might follow from a conviction. With the example of the northern abbots still fairly fresh in their minds it is hardly to be wondered at that they chose the safer course.

The fall of Lewes was followed, before the end of the year, by the surrender of two more houses, Titchfield in Hampshire and Warden in Bedfordshire, in each of which domestic discords probably contributed considerably to the willingness of the monks to resign. In January 1538 a few further surrenders followed and so began the long series of such surrenders which continued almost without interruption right through 1538, 1539 and the early months of 1540, ending only with the surrender of Waltham on 23 March in the latter year.

In the second place, not only did suppressions begin again, they also followed a significantly different pattern. Very much less emphasis was now placed upon the alleged iniquities of the religious and the pressing need for reform. The moral case which had been so prominent a part of the campaign against the lesser monasteries was now very much less in evidence. Instead the preambles to quite a number of the deeds of surrender spoke of the earnest desire of the religious to be released from a life of idleness and superstition.[1] The suppression act of 1536 had not attacked the monastic ideal itself, but had complained only of the failure of some of the monks and nuns to live up to the standards established by their own rules. The language of the surrender deeds went very much further when it asserted that the religious life, even when

'right well kept and observed'

was but a vain show and

'doth most principally consist in certain dumb ceremonies'

and so should be abandoned by all right-thinking men. No mere reform of the religious orders could hope to satisfy this sort of criticism. Total abolition alone would suffice.

That total abolition was indeed now the ultimate intention of the government was also strongly suggested by the abandonment of the former practice of offering the monks and nuns from dissolved houses the chance of continuing the religious life in another convent of the same order. From the time of the surrender of Lewes onwards this option was no longer made available. All the dispossessed religious were now retired on pension, and as the amount of such pensions was entirely at the discretion of the government this gave the suppressors a very helpful hold over the monks and nuns who did not take long to learn that a ready compliance with the wishes of the crown would be rewarded more generously than stubborn resistance to all persuasions.

---

[1] See the examples of surrender deeds given in the appendix to this chapter.

Rumours and Countermeasures

These hints of a change in government policy did not escape the attention of contemporary observers, and soon the view that all the abbeys were doomed was being widely expressed. Such rumours were not in themselves dangerous, for they did not seem to provoke the same degree of hostility as had those earlier rumours about the intended spoiling of the parish churches which had inflamed Lincolnshire in 1536 (above, p. 92). And yet the spreading of such notions could have undesirable consequences which the government was anxious to limit. In anticipation of a dissolution which now seemed to be only a matter of time some of the religious were strongly tempted to insure for the future by making profitable bargains with their secular neighbours. Leases could be granted on favourable terms; annuities could be sold cheaply or given away; the right of presentation to vicarages in the gift of the abbey could be alienated on the understanding that the new patron would give priority to former monks when vacancies occurred; abbey plate and other valuables could be converted into cash and the proceeds pocketed; in these and other ways the assets of a monastery could be realised before surrender and to the prejudice of the crown.

Anxious to prevent such happenings, Cromwell sent, in March 1538, a circular letter to the heads of all the remaining religious houses, assuring them that no general dissolution was intended, and that all the recent surrenders had been 'free and voluntary'. Furthermore, said Cromwell,

'his Grace's Highness hath commanded me for your repose to advertise you that unless there had been overtures made by the said houses that have resigned his Grace would never have received the same, and that his Majesty intendeth not in any wise to trouble you or to devise for the suppression of any religious house that standeth except they shall either desire of themselves with one whole consent to resist and forsake the same; or else misuse themselves contrary to their allegiance'.

This last phrase was both a reminder of the fate of the northern abbots and also a warning that any injudicious squandering of the abbey's assets might be so construed in future.

On the whole this warning circular probably had the desired effect of making the religious realise that it was more important for their future that they should satisfy the king and Cromwell by husbanding the resources of their houses than their neighbours by squandering them. Cases of collusive grants of leases and annuities are on record, but their number is not excessive when the total number of houses is borne in mind, and when the local pressures to which the religious were subjected are also remembered. Indeed, one enterprising Augmentations man, Leonard Beckwith, the Yorkshire receiver, whose duty it undoubtedly was to preserve as much monastic property as he could for the king's use, was not above using his official position to his own advantage. In 1538–9, when, as his enemies later alleged,

'it was perfectly known that the said houses should go down'

he made a most profitable tour of the remaining religious houses in his area, persuading no fewer than twenty-two of them, by

'reciting what he might do for them in their pensions and otherwise'

to make him grants of fees and annuities totalling no less than £54 a year.

Surrender by Negotiation

The process by which the greater abbeys and those which had secured exemption from the suppression statute fell to the crown was of necessity a lengthy one. Each surrender was the consequence of individual negotiations between the monks and the king's agents. Each community ended its own life by its own, theoretically voluntary, action. At no time was the government's intention of making an end of all the religious orders ever openly declared, and so at no time had the united opposition of the inhabitants of the surviving houses to be faced.

Some of the earlier surrenders were achieved only after quite protracted negotiations, for the government was at first inclined to move cautiously. Early in June 1538 the prior of Monk Bretton in Yorkshire was approached by Sir John Neville who was anxious to secure some of the priory's property for himself.

'I have been with the prior and he is almost at a point for the resignation of his house into the hands of the King's Highness'

wrote Sir John to Thomas Legh, but the point of resignation was not to be reached quite so easily as Neville had hoped, for in August the prior was still in possession and being subjected to further persuasions by William Blitheman, an Augmentations man, who hoped soon to be able to report success. But even Blitheman was too optimistic. For a further three months the prior held out, and it was not until 21 November that he and his brethren at last signed a deed of surrender.

It is possible that the surrender of another Yorkshire house, the Cistercian abbey of Byland, took even longer to negotiate. In March 1538 Thomas Legh visited the abbot, ostensibly to arrange about the grant of a lease to a client of Cromwell, but probably also to take soundings about a possible surrender. Shortly afterwards the abbot visited London, and the duke of Norfolk, who had clearly heard rumours about an impending surrender, wrote off urgently to Cromwell to ask him to spare the abbey as

'no house in these parts is more charged with hospitality'.

Byland eventually surrendered on 30 November.

By the autumn of 1538 the pace of the campaign was quickening. The rate of surrender, which in the earlier months of the year had seldom exceeded six a month, jumped in September to sixteen, and in October to nearly twenty. In part this was due to the coming to fruition of lengthy negotiations commenced in the spring, but it was also the consequence of an improvement in the techniques of persuasion which some of Cromwell's more skilful, or more ruthless, agents had now brought to such a pitch that they were able in the course of comparatively brief tours to clear selected parts of the country of virtually all their remaining monasteries.

One very effective local sweep was made through Staffordshire by Thomas Legh. In five days in mid-September he secured the surrenders of Tutbury, Rocester, Croxden and Hulton. In the following month another five-day trip resulted in four further surrenders in Staffordshire and neighbouring Shropshire. Legh then passed into Derbyshire where Darley, Dale and Repton all yielded to his persuasions within the space of a further four days. Meanwhile William Petre had been equally busy in Lincolnshire and Nottinghamshire where in just over a fortnight he had taken the surrenders of no less than nine houses of the Gilbertine order which had its greatest strength in that part of the country, and had by then been deprived of its former immunity.

Perhaps the most remarkable, and, from the crown's point of view, the most fruitful of these local sweeps was that made through Gloucestershire, Wiltshire, Dorset, Somerset, Devon and Cornwall by Petre and John Tregonwell in the early months of 1539. Setting out in January, they scored their first success at Poulton in Gloucestershire on the 16th. By the end of the month they were well into Somerset. By 16 February they had crossed into Devon, whence, after a brief incursion into Cornwall, they returned through Dorset to Wiltshire in March. By 1 April they had secured between them no fewer than forty surrenders and had left hardly a house standing in the whole of the south-west.

The Methods Employed

A good idea of the methods which might be employed on these surrender-seeking tours is given by the instructions issued for the guidance of the team of commissioners charged in November 1539 with the dissolution of all the remaining houses in Staffordshire, Shropshire, Cheshire, Yorkshire, Cumberland, Northumberland and Durham. Headed by Walter Hendle, the Solicitor of the court of Augmentations, and including both Richard Layton and Thomas Legh, this group was to make the last great suppression-sweep on record. Starting with Burton-on-Trent on 14 November, they moved swiftly into Yorkshire where in a little over a month some seventeen abbeys surrendered to them. Durham came next, then Northumberland and Cumberland. They were at Carlisle on 9 January 1540. From there they returned through Lancashire to Cheshire and Shropshire, and the last surrender to their credit is that of Wenlock on 26 January. By then the process of dissolution was complete in the north, and only a handful of abbeys was left elsewhere.

The instructions which these northern commissioners carried with them were quite explicit. They were to suppress or alter *all* the religious houses yet remaining in their area. There were to be no exceptions or exemptions. The only alternative to suppression which was now permitted was 'alteration' by which was meant the secularisation and continuation of an existing monastic cathedral chapter, as at Durham, the creation of a new cathedral out of an existing abbey, as at Chester, or the conversion of an abbey into a collegiate church, as at Burton-on-Trent. But only a few houses were to be thus altered, and none was to have any voice in the determination of its own fate.

In this important matter not even the commissioners were to have any discretion. They were to take with them a previously prepared 'book' of all the religious houses within their commission, and this 'book' would instruct them how to proceed in each case. The whole operation was planned in advance, and it is clear that no effective opposition to the commissioners' proceedings was anticipated.

The fact that the fate of every house had already been settled before the commissioners had set out on their journey was not, of course, known to the religious in their area, and some did make an effort to preserve their houses from destruction. On 9 November, as the comsioners were journeying northwards, William Thornton, the abbot of St. Mary's York, wrote to Cromwell to plead for the continuation of his abbey, with 'some alteration' to meet the king's wishes. Five days later he went further and, repeating his former request, dispatched his prior and another monk to London to press the matter in person. And yet, even as he made his plea for the preservation of his house, abbot Thornton can have entertained but little hope of success. What chance had even his great abbey of survival in opposition to the minster at York? There was no room in that city for a new cathedral, or even for a collegiate church. So little real hope of success had Thornton that in the very letter in which he asked that his abbey might be spared he was careful to name the particular monastic manor to which he would prefer to retire should St. Mary's be dissolved. In the event the abbot's letters were ignored, and when the commissioners reached his doors on 29 November they found him and all his brethren 'very obedient' and ready to accept with a good grace a fate that was clearly inescapable.

The 'obedience' of the abbot and monks of York is not so surprising when we consider further the nature of the instructions upon which Hendle and his fellow commissioners were required to act. All abbeys which were not marked down for 'alteration' were forthwith to be dissolved

> 'taking the consent of the heads and convents by way of their free surrender under the convent seal . . . if they will thereunto willingly consent and agree'

in which case the commissioners were to treat the monks generously, to award them pensions and dispense gratuities to cover the cost of their new secular apparel, and also to divide their household goods among them

'after the rate of their revenues and possessions of the houses and the qualities of the persons'.

If, however, the monks or nuns were not willing to co-operate thus freely, their lands and possessions were to be seized to the king's use, and though they were still to get some money to help with the purchase of secular apparel, 'such obstinate and wilful persons' were to be granted no pensions until the king's further pleasure was known. Finally, any who still declined to yield to the will of the commissioners were to be committed for punishment as time and opportunity provided.

Further Executions

What this last phrase might mean must have been only too clear to those of the religious who had observed the fate of the priory of Lenton and the abbey of Woburn in 1538, and the more recent, but very similar, cases of Colchester, Reading and Glastonbury in the autumn of 1539. These five houses were not surrendered. They came to the crown by forfeiture after the condemnation and execution of their heads. The charges against the four abbots and the prior varied. Abbot Whiting of Glastonbury was in the end accused of robbing his own abbey of its treasures, the others died for various alleged treasons, the details of which are in some cases obscure. It is, however, difficult to avoid the conclusion that a contributory cause of their condemnation was their reluctance to surrender their abbeys. The abbot of Woburn, even at the very end, continued to maintain his disapproval of the dissolution, and the abbot of Colchester had gone even further and said openly that the

'King's grace could not at any time lawfully nor by any law suppress any house of religion that were above the yearly value of three hundred marks (= £200), saying also that he should never surrender up his house and lands to the King's hands, saying then also that he had as lief die as to forsake his living, saying also that it could not stand with his conscience to forsake his house'.

Though it was not for these words alone that he was condemned to die it is still open to us to doubt whether, had the abbot been more willing to meet the king's wishes in the matter of surrender, the other charges against him would have been proceeded with.

At the time of the abbot of Colchester's arrest and trial, in November 1539, the northern suppression commissioners had not for long been embarked upon their tour. The execution of the abbot on 1 December, and the similar fate suffered by the abbots of Reading and Glastonbury in the previous month, cannot have been entirely without influence upon the attitude of the inhabitants of the surviving abbeys. By their instructions which they carried with them on their surrender-seeking tour of the north, Hendle and his fellow commissioners were, as we have seen (above, pp. 113–4), required to use blandishments and persuasions before they turned to threats, but such threats can seldom have been necessary. Bearing in mind the fate of the few who had shown reluctance to surrender, most of the other religious were as eager to show themselves 'obedient' as were the monks of York. The time for a united stand, if any indeed had had the heart for it, was long past.

The Friars: Visitation

At the same time as the suppression of the larger abbeys was in train, the agents of the government were also turning their attention to another group of religious houses which had not been covered by the dissolution act, the 180 or so houses of the mendicant friars, scattered throughout the principal towns up and down the country. That they were dealt with in the same way and at the same time as the larger abbeys does seem to confirm what we suggested above (p. 108) that by 1538 the very ideal of the monastic life, and not simply the inadequate expression given to it by some of the monks and nuns, was under attack. The property of the friaries was no great prize for the government to lay its hands on, and cannot stand comparison with that of the monks. Their urban sites, some with orchards and gardens attached, were their chief assets, and were, in some instances, eagerly sought after by would-be purchasers, but, apart from these, the friaries possessed little of value save the lead on their roofs and the plate on their altars. They owned no manors, rectories or granges, and very few other endowments, and depended almost entirely upon the charity of the local people for their sustenance. This latter source of income was now, according to the testimony of the friars themselves, drying up, so that many of them were glad enough, when the time came, to change their habits and embark upon new careers.

Nor was the loyalty of the friars in question. Those of them who had opposed the new régime and declined to take the oaths of succession and supremacy, principally the Observant branch of the Franciscan order, had been dealt with in barbarous fashion in 1534; the rest had submitted as readily as the majority of the monks. Indeed, some of the friars, far from being secret supporters of the papacy, must be numbered among the most outspoken and ardent advocates of religious innovations more sweeping than any that the king was prepared to allow. Robert Barnes, whose preaching led him to a heretic's death in 1540, Miles Coverdale, translator of the Bible and later protestant bishop of Exeter, and John Bale, protestant litterateur and controversialist, were but three of the best-known friars of this stamp. It was hardly as potential papalists that the friars were suppressed. Yet suppressed they had to be, for it clearly would have been inconsistent to have proceeded with the dissolution of the greater abbeys and nunneries on the grounds that their lives were vain and superstitious, and yet to have left the friars in their houses and habits. If the monks went, the friars would have to go too.

The agent to whom the task of disposing of the friaries was principally committed was himself a former friar and ex-provincial of the Dominicans, Richard Ingworth, suffragan bishop of Dover, who was appointed by royal authority to be visitor-general of the mendicant orders on 6 February 1538. The work of suppression, which began in the midlands in the spring, at first proceeded slowly, for Ingworth himself seemed to be uncertain as to what was expected of him. Normally it was not the task of a visitor to press for surrenders, but only to issue injunctions for the amendment of life and the better observation of the rule. On 5 May the visitor received a second commission which enlarged his authority by empowering him to draw up inventories of the goods and possessions of the friaries he visited, and to put their plate and other valuables in safe keeping so that the friars could not sell or conceal them. These new powers the bishop of Dover soon used to good effect. No longer supported by the alms of the local people, and now debarred by the visitor's action from raising money by pawning or selling their valuables, the friars, as Ingworth repeatedly claimed in his letters to Cromwell, would soon be forced by their very poverty to surrender their houses to the king.

9 Newstead: an Augustinian priory in Nottinghamshire, converted into a residence immediately after the dissolution. Of the church only the western façade now stands. The cloister has suffered alteration at the hands of later owners, but much of the original fabric and plan survives. This view is taken from the west

10 Buckland: the church of this Devonshire Cistercian abbey has been converted into a dwelling house. This view, from the south-west, shows the nave, tower and south transept. The cloister lay on the north side of the church and has entirely disappeared

The censer and incense boat shown here are two of the very few pieces of monastic silver to have escaped destruction at the dissolution. They were found, in company with a number of pewter plates, when Whittlesey Mere in Huntingdonshire was drained in 1850. The rams' heads rising from the waves at either end of the incense boat show that it came from nearby Ramsey Abbey. Both pieces are now in the Victoria and Albert Museum

11 The Ramsey Abbey Censer

12 The Ramsey Abbey Incense Boat

The Friars: Suppression

But Cromwell was not satisfied. The slowness of this method of starving the friars into surrender did not appeal to his brisk mind. In a letter not now extant, but whose contents we can infer from the terms of Ingworth's reply on 28 July, the king's vicar-general insisted upon the adoption of more forceful methods and the securing of speedier results. The bishop of Dover's response to this rebuke was immediate and striking. Whereas during his tours of the midlands in May and of Sussex, Hampshire and Wiltshire in June and July he had acted primarily as visitor and had been content to leave many friars in possession because he found their houses 'in good order', from August onwards, as he moved through the west country, into Wales, and then, in September, through the south-west, he acted almost exclusively the part of the suppressor, and the surrenders came in thick and fast.

Ingworth had been made to realise at last that, whatever the formal wording of his commission as visitor, it was the securing of surrenders and not reform of misliving that was expected of him. He had still, however, no authority directly to demand surrenders, or to effect suppressions against the wills of the friars themselves, but he soon devised a sophisticated technique which enabled him in most cases successfully to surmount this technical difficulty. Appearing in the guise of visitor, and disclaiming any desire to act as suppressor, he would freely and magnanimously offer to the brethren at each friary the choice between being released from their vows to seek their fortune in the secular world and remaining in their habits and observing faithfully such injunctions as he would give them. He would then recite the proposed injunctions which would have bound the friars to a far stricter adherence to the rules of their orders than that to which they had been for so many years accustomed. Faced with this choice most of the friars speedily decided to surrender their houses and to leave off their habits. They were unable with any justice to complain of the severity of the proposed injunctions. They were equally clear that they could hardly undertake to observe them to the letter.

Only exceptionally, as with the Black Friars of Shrewsbury, did this gambit of Ingworth's not produce immediate success, and by the end of 1538 he had dispatched practically all the friars in the west and south. Meanwhile John London, warden of New College Oxford,

I

had been busy dealing with the friars in his own university town, with those at Reading and in Warwickshire and Northamptonshire. John Hilsey, an ex-Dominican, and now successor to John Fisher in the see of Rochester, had dealt with Cambridge, and the duke of Norfolk and others had also taken a hand. In February and March of 1539 the remaining friaries, mostly in Lincolnshire and the north, were dealt with by the bishop of Dover, and the suppression of the mendicants in England and Wales was then complete.

For a year longer the campaign against the larger abbeys, which had begun a little before the attack on the friaries and had been running concurrently with it, continued. In March 1540 the last abbey surrendered and the religious orders in England and Wales were at last extinct.

APPENDIX: DEEDS OF SURRENDER

(From Rymer's *Foedera*, vol. XIV, pp. 610–11. Spelling modernised. The Cistercian abbey of Biddlesden in Buckinghamshire was assessed in the *Valor Ecclesiasticus* at £125 and so was liable to suppression under the statute of 1536. It was, however, granted exemption from suppression by letters patent dated 17 August 1536. Thereafter it was treated in the same manner as any of the larger abbeys which had never come within the scope of the suppression act, and when it eventually fell in September 1538, it was by virtue of the 'voluntary' act of surrender quoted here. The surrender of the Grey Friars of Bedford is given here as an example of quite a number of surrenders of friaries which are couched in virtually identical language and are clearly copies of an exemplar carried by the suppressors. Notice the close correspondence between the two surrenders which suggests that the Biddlesden text was also the work of a government pen. Notice too the emphasis placed upon the vanity of the regular life.)

1 THE SURRENDER OF THE ABBOT AND MONKS OF BIDDLESDEN

Forasmuch as we, Richard Grene, abbot of the Monastery of Our Blessed Lady Saint Mary of Biddlesden, and the convent of the same monastery do profoundly consider that the manner and trade of living which we and other of our pretensed religion have practised and used many days doth most principally consist in certain dumb ceremonies and in certain constitutions of Rome and other forinsecal potentates, as the abbot of Citeaux and other in only no solid and not taught in the true knowledge of God's laws, procuring always principally to forinsecal potentates and powers which never came here to reform such discord of living and abuses as now have been found to have reigned among us, and therefore, now assuredly knowing that the most perfect way of living is most principally and sufficiently declared unto us by our master Christ, his evangelists and apostles, and that is most expedient for us to be governed and ordered by our own Supreme Head under God, the King's most noble grace, with our mutual assent and consent do most humbly submit ourself and every one of us unto the most benign mercy of the King's Majesty, and by these presents do surrender and yield up unto his most gracious hands all our said monastery, with all the lands spiritual and temporal, tithes, rents, reversions, rights and revenues we have in all and every part of the same, most humbly beseeching his Grace so to dispose of us and of the same as shall seem best unto his most gracious pleasure.

And further in like humble manner desiring his most noble Grace to grant unto every one of us under his letters patent some annuity or other manner of living whereby we may be assured to have our sustenance in time coming.

And further to grant unto us freely his licence to change our habits into secular fashion, and to receive such manner of living as other secular priests be wont to have, and all we and every one of us shall faithfully pray unto Almighty God long to preserve his Grace with increase of much felicity.

In witness whereof we have subscribed our names and put our convent seal unto these presents the 25 day of September in the thirtieth year of the reign of our sovereign lord King Henry the Eighth.

2. THE SURRENDER OF THE GREY FRIARS OF BEDFORD

Forasmuch as we, the Warden and friars of the house of Saint Francis in Bedford in the county of Bedford, do profoundly consider that the perfection of Christian living doth not consist in dumb ceremonies, wearing of a grey coat, disguising ourself after strange fashions, ducking and becking, in girding ourselves with a girdle full of knots, and other like papistical ceremonies, wherein we have been most principally practised and misled in times past, but the very true way to please God and to live a true Christian man without all hypocrisy and feigned dissimulation is sincerely declared unto us by our Master Christ, his evangelists and apostles; being minded hereafter to follow the same, conforming our self unto the will and pleasure of our Supreme Head under God in earth, the King's Majesty, and not to follow henceforth the superstitious traditions of any forinsecal potentate or power, with mutual assent and consent do submit ourselves unto the mercy of our said Sovereign Lord, and with like mutual assent and consent do surrender &c.

And in witness of all and singular the premises, we, the said Warden and convent of the Grey Friars in Bedford to these presents have put our convent seal the third day of October in the thirtieth year of the reign of our most Sovereign Lord King Henry the Eighth.

Section III

The Aftermath

9

The Realisation of the Properties

BY the spring of 1540 the religious orders in England and Wales were no more, and their lands, buildings, farmstock and furnishings had all passed into the hands of the crown. Had Henry VIII been able, or inclined, to retain in full possession this enormous mass of property, the subsequent course of English history might well have been very different. Had the wealth of the monasteries been so managed as to have formed a permanent addition to the endowments of the crown, it would almost certainly have freed king Henry and his immediate successors from that steadily increasing dependence upon the financial assistance of parliament which was to result, in the long run, in the eroding away of royal power and the establishment of parliamentary supremacy.

The Profit to the Crown

The total annual net income of the religious orders had been assessed in 1535 by the commissioners for the Tenth at a little over £136,000,[1] but, because of omissions from and underestimates in their survey the true figure was probably nearer to £175,000, or nearly three quarters as much again as the average annual income of the crown at the same date. It might therefore be supposed that the seizure by the crown of the property of the religious orders should have had the result of nearly trebling its ordinary revenues, but this happy state of affairs was not even momentarily reached. At no one point of time did the king ever hold the entire assets of all the religious houses in his hands. The process of disposal began before the process of acquisition was complete. Furthermore, although the estimates of

---

[1] The figures given on p. 3 above were of gross income.

net income compiled by the Tenths commissioners made allowance for the fees of the lay administrators of monastic estates, which the crown continued to pay after the dissolution, they naturally took no account of the additional commitments which were undertaken by the government at the time of the suppression. Pensions were assigned to the dispossessed religious, annuities granted by the monks were honoured and creditors were satisfied, and all these outgoings were charged against the income from the monastic estates. The burden of such liabilities was often substantial. Indeed, in some extreme cases the crown was initially committed to paying out more than the value of the property from which the charges arose. Cases in point are the four small Yorkshire priories whose balance sheet for the year Michaelmas 1541 to Michaelmas 1542 is shown in the following table:

House	Net value for Tenth in 1535			Rents received 1541/2			Cost of pensions, fees, etc.			Repairs to property			Net actual loss to crown		
	£	s.	d.	£	s.	d.	£	s.	d.	£	s.	d.	£	s.	d.
Arthington	11	8	4½	21	2	0	23	3	4		nil		2	1	4
Baysdale	20	1	4	26	11	0	29	0	0		15	0	3	4	0
Nunkeeling	35	15	5	26	7	6	36	5	0		nil		9	17	6
Thicket	20	18	10	20	15	6	19	0	0	3	15	0	1	19	6
Totals	£88	3	11½	£94	16	0	£107	8	4	£4	10	0	£17	2	4

Thus, where the figures of the Tenths commissioners would suggest a gain to the crown of more than £88 it was in fact experiencing a loss of over £17. Of course these four small priories have been deliberately selected as extreme cases, and must not be taken as typical, but they do serve to remind us rather pointedly that the Tenths commissioners' returns are by no means as reliable a guide to the profit made by the crown at the time of the dissolution as might at first sight be supposed. On the other hand it must be remembered that pensions, annuities and fees were not perpetual charges upon the monastic estates, and that their amount would be progressively diminished as the years passed and the beneficiaries died off, so that, in the long run, and if it had not meantime disposed of the properties, the crown would come to enjoy from them an income even greater than that shown in the returns of the Tenths commissioners.

The Rate of Disposal

The government could not, however, afford to wait for these long-term benefits of the dissolution to be felt. From the very first the need for ready money was pressing, and, with the outbreak of war with Scotland in 1542 and with France in 1543, became more pressing still. This last war of Henry VIII's reign was by far the most expensive. One estimate puts its total cost at over £2,000,000, more than eleven times the Tenth commissioners' estimate of the annual value of all the monastic properties. And even before the outbreak of the war considerable sums had been spent upon improving and repairing defensive fortifications along the south coast and the Scottish border. The government needed large sums quickly, and the only way that these could be raised was by outright sales of monastic lands.

There is some evidence to suggest that Cromwell himself was not in favour of such sales and would have liked to have kept the monastic properties intact as a permanent endowment for the crown, but he did not live long enough to have any substantial influence upon the policy of disposal. Before his fall in 1540 he had seemed to favour leases rather than sales, and, though he and the chancellor of Augmentations were empowered, in December 1539, to sell lands on behalf of the crown, few such sales took place while Cromwell was alive. And yet it must also be said that the real spate of sales did not begin until 1543, some three years after Cromwell's disgrace and execution, so that it is quite legitimate to suggest that it was the outbreak of war rather than the fall of the great minister which really caused the change in policy. Be that as it may, the years 1543–7 saw the disposal by sale of something like two-thirds of all the monastic estates. What was left in the king's hands at the end of his reign was far from being sufficient to give the crown that financial independence which Cromwell had probably planned for it to have. The immediate crisis of the 1540s had been surmounted, but the government was once again on the verge of bankruptcy. The proceeds of the dissolution had certainly helped to carry the crown through a critical decade, but had brought it no substantial permanent endowment. Throughout the troubled years of Edward and Mary, and well into Elizabeth's reign, monastic lands continued to be sold whenever the crown was short of money. By the reign of James I there was little left to sell, and the ultimate dependence of the crown upon parliamentary supply was becoming painfully obvious.

When we write or speak of the 'monastic lands' or 'monastic estates' we generally refer to that wide range of indestructible assets which the religious orders possessed. We include not only the sites upon which the actual monasteries stood, with their gardens surrounding them and demesne lands close by, but also their outlying granges and manors (many of them let on long leases), their scattered urban lots, their title to the tithes of appropriated churches, their right of presentation to incumbencies in their gift, and many other miscellaneous perquisites such as the abbot of Whitby's right to wrecks along the coast near by. All these were sources of regular income, and marketable commodities. All brought profit to the crown as long as it kept possession, and fetched a good price when the time came to sell them. But there were other assets of a rather different kind which also came to the king's hand as a consequence of the dissolution; the actual churches and claustral buildings with all their furnishings and equipment, and the farm stock and implements employed upon the demesne. These too had their price and were readily saleable, but could not very easily be made to yield a permanent income. Indeed they would probably realise most if sold immediately, before deterioration had set in.

The Buildings and Furnishings

The more valuable and imperishable metals were generally given first priority by the suppressors and immediately secured for the use of the crown. All gold and silver vessels, plate and ornaments were carefully inventoried and sent off to the King's jewel house where some of the finest pieces were preserved for the King's personal use while the rest were added to the royal stock of bullion, ready to be melted down and coined, or sold to raise cash. The total value of all the gold, silver and jewels obtained from the dissolution of the monasteries and the pulling down of the shrines that many of them housed was at least £75,000, but this figure represents the value of the metal and stones assessed by weight alone, and takes no account of the artistic worth of the many chalices, flagons, dishes, crosses, candlesticks and other items thus destroyed.

Equally carefully inventoried by the suppressors were the church bells of which even the humblest priory would have at least one to summon the monks or nuns to their daily devotions. The greater abbeys often possessed extensive peals. Bell metal, being a sturdy rust-resistant alloy of copper and tin was in great demand for the manufacture of cannon which were coming to be needed in ever increasing numbers not only as siege weapons or for the manning of defensive works, but also to arm the new-style fighting ships which sought to destroy their opponents at long range by gunfire instead of closing with them and grappling and boarding. Many of the abbey bells therefore found their way to the foundry in the Tower of London whence they soon reappeared in their new military guise.

Almost as valuable a prize as the abbey bells was the great quantity of lead which lined the gutters and in many cases sheathed the roofs of the abbey churches and principal conventual buildings. As the appendix to Chapter 6 showed, the suppression commissioners in their descriptions of priory buildings were always careful to specify the type of roofing material used. Thatch and slates had little value, but lead, although a native English mineral, had then, as now, in its refined state, a considerable scarcity value. All the available lead was therefore stripped from the roofs of all those monastic buildings which were considered superfluous to the needs of the new occupants. The process of removal was often a lengthy one, for the lead sheeting had to be melted down and recast into pigs to facilitate transport, and labour skilled enough to perform this operation on the site itself was sometimes difficult to find.

In Yorkshire, the lead from the roofs of the smaller abbeys was dealt with by a team of local men during the course of 1537 and the early months of 1538. Their method of working was not very efficient and involved a double process. First the lead itself was melted in pits in the ground, and then the ashes left over from this process were further refined in order to extract from them additional supplies of metal which might otherwise have been lost. When the larger monasteries came to be dealt with the task was entrusted to a French expert (with the very English name of Henry Johnson) whose commission, dated 20 March 1539, required him to supervise the melting process throughout the north, and in many midland counties too. His methods, which involved the construction of proper furnaces, proved so much more efficient that he was able to omit the supplementary refining of the ashes. The pigs of lead were, where possible, transported by water, and York and Hull were the gathering points for supplies from the north, some of which went thence by sea to London, and some directly to the Netherlands.

The removal of the roofing lead was almost invariably accompanied by the pulling down of the roof timbers to use as fuel for melting it. The churches and other buildings so unroofed were thus exposed to the eroding influences of the weather, and needed no more than continual neglect to reduce them to the ruinous state in which we find so many of them today. In some parts of the country, notably in Lincolnshire, the work of destruction was deliberately carried further, and whole abbeys were demolished completely immediately after suppression, so that only the foundations were left to mark the outlines and dimensions of the former buildings. Such demolitions, however, often involved a considerable expenditure of time and energy, for the monks had built solidly and well, and it could sometimes cost more to demolish an abbey than the value of the building stone which could be salvaged and sold. Total demolition was not therefore generally resorted to, indeed there was no national uniformity in the treatment meted out to the buildings of suppressed monasteries, and quite a number of monastic churches have survived in whole or in part to the present day.

Surviving Buildings

Best known of monastic survivals are the fourteen cathedrals which once did duty as the churches of great monasteries. Eight of these, Canterbury, Durham, Worcester, Winchester, Rochester, Ely, Norwich and Carlisle, had been seats of bishops for centuries before the dissolution. They ceased now to be monasteries, but continued as cathedrals, with their monastic chapters secularised. Their fabric was left untouched, their churches have survived intact with, in many cases, the monastic cloister still attached, though the buildings around the cloister have in most cases suffered considerable alteration to adapt them to the very different needs of secular canons who no longer shared a common life, and, from the reign of Elizabeth onwards, were no longer required to be celibate. Six other large monastic churches, at Westminster, Bristol, Oxford, Gloucester, Peterborough and Chester, were also preserved from destruction to act as the cathedral churches of the new sees created by Henry VIII. This again meant the preservation not only of the churches but also of a proportion of the other monastic buildings according to the needs of the secularised chapter.

To these well-known monastic survivals can be added quite a number of others. In some places where the monks' church had also served the needs of the local community it was not entirely destroyed and some portion of it, generally the nave, remained, and still remains in use as the parish church. Examples of this kind of survival may be seen at Bolton (Yorks.), Malmesbury (Wilts.), Binham (Norfolk) and Ewenny (Glamorgan). Elsewhere one occasionally finds, as at Beaulieu (Hants.), that although the monks' church is in ruins some other part of the conventual buildings (at Beaulieu the frater) has been preserved by conversion to use as a church. Exceptionally, as at Buckland (Devon), parts of the monks' church have been converted into a residence, almost completely disguising its original character.

More usually, however, it is the church which has fallen into decay, or has been completely destroyed, while other parts of the monastic complex have been preserved by conversion into a dwelling for the new owner. Good examples of such conversions which have preserved the original lines of the cloister and much of the fabric of the buildings surrounding it may be seen at Newstead (Notts.) and Lacock (Wilts.). At Lanercost (Cumberland), the western range of the cloister proved adequate for the needs of the new owner, and the rest was allowed to fall into ruins, save for the nave of the church which was retained in use by the parish. At Forde (Dorset) the monks' dorter and frater, the abbot's lodging, the chapter house and the portion of the cloister connecting them formed the nucleus of a great house built in the seventeenth century, but the rest of the site was cleared. At Hinton (Somerset) it was the gatehouse which was converted into a residence. The variations in treatment are numerous, and these few examples must suffice to give some idea of the different ways in which the purchasers of monastic sites might choose to adapt the buildings which came into their possession.

There were, of course, some who made no attempt at conversion but, like Cromwell's nephew at Lewes, preferred to pull down the existing buildings and use the materials from them to erect a completely new structure. Others, while not destroying the old fabric entirely, used it as a quarry for building stone, and left what they did not need to weather and decay. But in every case the value of the monastic buildings was included in the purchase price of the site, and if any lead was left in place on roofs or gutters, that also had to be valued and paid for by the new owner.

The Disposal of Furnishings

The interior furnishings of the abbeys were also put up for sale, and everything that could possibly be put to profitable use, from the monks' stalls in the abbey church down to the simplest pot-hook in the monastery kitchen, was sold for the best price that it would fetch. The new occupier of the premises, be he only temporary farmer, more permanent lessee or perpetual grantee, was generally given first option on such items as might be of use to him. He usually purchased any livestock and farm implements available, for he would want to take over the monks' demesne farm as a going concern, and not to have to stock it for himself. But even when the farmer had taken his pick there were, as a general rule, still plenty of bargains to be had, and not much was overlooked.

A few books from monastic libraries, mainly those with an antiquarian interest, were preserved for the royal collection which later was to become one of the nuclei of the British Museum Library, but countless others were disposed of for the sake of their parchment and vellum alone, without regard to the interest or value of their contents, or the beauty of their calligraphy or illumination. At Roche (Yorks.) it was said that some of the local carters found the monks' service books useful for mending the holes in the coverings of their wagons, but at nearby Monk Bretton the monks prized their library more highly and a group of them managed to secure nearly 150 books for themselves by purchase. Embroidered copes and other vestments, unless they had a high intrinsic value because of the use of metalled threads, were also sold for what they would fetch, and some found new employment as bed hanging or coverlet.

The sums of money raised by such sales of abbey buildings, furnishings and stock were in total considerable, and during the early years, immediately after the dissolution, probably exceeded by a considerable margin the income derived from the rental value of the newly-acquired estates. Precise figures for the whole country have not yet been worked out. The central records, the accounts of the treasurer of the court of Augmentations, do give the value of the plate and jewels sent up to London by the suppressors, but the amounts raised locally by the sale of furnishings and stock can only be determined from the local records, the accounts of the seventeen particular receivers, each responsible for the realisation of the monastic assets in his own area, and the figures from these sources remain to be gathered up. Meanwhile the best we can do is to give a few sample figures from the surviving accounts for a single area, Yorkshire, which show what was probably the general trend.

Year of account	Value of jewels and plate and proceeds from sale of goods, etc.	Income from rents	Total income
	£	£	£
1536	3,102	186	3,288
1538–9	1,639	3,200	4,839
1541–2	158	11,061	11,219
1544–5	149	8,837	8,986

In 1536 only the first few small houses had been dissolved, and rents were received for only a few months. In 1538–9 some of the larger abbeys had surrendered, and the account covered a complete financial year. The rent roll is consequently considerably larger, though the proceeds from the sale of goods still account for a substantial proportion of the total income. Were the account for 1539–40 now extant it would probably show a much larger figure for such sales, as it was in that year that the majority of the greater houses in Yorkshire surrendered. The account for 1541–2 shows the rent roll at its maximum before sales of land had made any substantial inroads upon it. Something is still being raised by the sale of movable goods, but in proportion to the amount now being received in rents this source of income has shrunk to insignificance. The last account, that for 1544–5, sees the rent roll beginning to contract as sales take effect.

The Sale of Lands

It is to these sales that we must now turn our attention. The old notion that many estates were given away, or sold at nominal prices to court favourites, has long since been shown to be untenable. While it is true that a few favoured aristocrats, notably the king's brother-in-law the duke of Suffolk, and his faithful and able servants secretary Cromwell and chancellor Audley, were the recipients of substantial grants on very favourable terms, it is equally true that such con-cessionary grants were the exception and that the main bulk of the monastic properties was sold at what was currently accepted as the fair price for land, namely 'twenty years' purchase' (i.e. a sum equal to twenty times the estimated annual yield from rents.)[2] At this price there seems to have been a steady demand for land which even the extensive sales of the 1540s do not appear to have satisfied, for there was no appreciable falling off in price even during the peak period of sales during the course of the war.

Who then were the purchasers who were so ready to come forward and buy all that the crown chose to offer? It is not easy to fit them into neat categories for they are such a heterogeneous lot, drawn from such a wide range of social classes. Some were already great land-owners, and peers, who wished to add to their already extensive estates. Others were younger sons of landed families who were mak-ing their way in the law or in the service of the government and wel-comed the opportunity of creating an independent establishment for themselves among the landed families from which they sprang. Others, generally purchasers of small or isolated lots, were prosper-ous yeomen, perhaps glad to have the chance to buy the freehold of land which they already held on lease. Some few were city folk who bought up rents as investments, but on the whole there was no great or sudden emergence of a new class of landlords. Most purchasers came from landed stock, even if at the time of making their purchase they happened to be engaged in trade or following a profession.

Very few indeed were the commercially-minded rackrenting absentee landlords who sometimes play so large a part in sentimental and unhistorical accounts of the dissolution. Probably non-existent too were the large-scale speculators who would not have had many opportunities for profit-taking in a decade when the price of land remained so stable. The groups of London merchants who entered the market in the mid-40s, purchased extensive lots of monastic properties, and resold them piecemeal almost at once, were in all like-lihood agents working on commission for provincial clients who were thus spared the expense and inconvenience of a journey to the capital to negotiate their purchases for themselves. Very frequently the pro-perties purchased by these syndicates were heterogeneous collections

---

[2] For a full examination of the post-dissolution market in monastic lands see the important article by H. J. Habakkuk in *Economic History Review*, vol. X, 1958.

of odd items, a single house lot in a town, a cottage with a few acres, the tithe of a single church, which were unlikely to appeal to the bigger investor but could be readily disposed of to local purchasers.

And yet the present tendency to transform all those who formerly were regarded as speculators into honest brokers must not be allowed to go too far. There is at least one fully documented case of un-doubted speculation where an enterprising middleman, buying on deferred terms, resold at a profit of nearly 23% before the original purchase money became due.[3] He might indeed have done even better had not illness hampered his activities. It is only the chance that the man who bought the property from him was later accused of fraud-ulent dealings which brought this speculator into court as a witness and preserved his story for us in the records of the case. Other similar deals may have left no record. It is hard to believe that only one man in all England saw and seized the chance to get rich quickly in this way. Contemporary techniques of survey and valuation were far from accurate, especially when it came to estimating the value of standing timber. Here and there in the record we get hints that men with specialised local knowledge were quick to notice and to take advantage of any serious undervaluation of monastic property by the officials of the court of Augmentations. The sheer bulk of the work entailed in surveying and valuing the properties which were dis-posed of in such numbers in the 1540s must have resulted in quite a number of such undervaluations and have provided many with opportunities for rapid profit-taking.

No Revolutionary Change

Some fortunes were undoubtedly made out of the dissolution, but not many, and certainly not a sufficient number to justify any belief in the emergence of a new-rich class. On balance the effect of the great transfer of property was not revolutionary. The secular landed classes, the aristocracy and the gentry, increased their acreage at the expense of the church, but the structure of, and balance of forces within secular society itself, were little affected. The 'new' landlords were the old, or their near relations, sharing much the same outlook, and similar ideas on estate management. There was no sudden or dramatic change in the attitude of landlords towards their tenants.

[3] For the details of this interesting case see G. W. O. Woodward, 'A Speculation in Monastic Lands' in *English Historical Review*, vol. LXXIX, 1964.

Under the continuing pressure of inflation rents were certainly rising in the years after the dissolution, but they rose no faster on estates which had once belonged to the monasteries than they did on others which had long been in lay hands, and in some parts of the country rents had, in any case, been rising for many years before the suppression. As the abbots' record as landlords had been no better and no worse than that of their lay contemporaries, so, now that the abbots had gone, there was nothing to distinguish the management techniques of their successors from those of their neighbours. The notion that kind-hearted, charitable and easy-going monastic land-lords were as a result of the dissolution replaced by harsh, unfeeling, profit-dominated 'new men' is not supported by the evidence.

Nor is there any distinction to be drawn between a 'protestant' and a 'catholic' attitude towards the purchase of lands once devoted to the maintenance of the religious orders. For men of all religious sympathies such purchases were straightforward business deals into which considerations of faith or sentiment did not enter, and among the biggest buyers of monastic lands are to be found as frequently those who later became recusants as those who became puritans. To say that by selling off the property of the monasteries Henry VIII 'created a vested interest in the reformation' is to misrepresent the truth. The members of the house of Commons in Mary's third parliament, who were ready enough to restore the papal supremacy, nevertheless refused to entertain any proposals for the restoration of the properties of the religious orders. In so doing they were not necessarily displaying their protestant sympathies, but merely their good business sense. During the course of the dissolution, as we have seen, every care had been taken to provide adequate compensation for all those whose interests might be in any way adversely affected. Furthermore the great majority of those who had subsequently come into possession of monastic properties had done so as the result of purchases made in good faith and paid for with good money. Consequently any scheme for the restoration of the religious orders would have to include proper compensation for all those who would be required to give up their estates. But where could money for the payment of such compensation be obtained, save from taxation? And so if the queen wished to repurchase monastic lands in order to re-endow the religious orders, she could only do so by imposing a substantial tax upon her subjects. What member of parliament, whatever his

K

religious sympathies, would readily have supported a proposal to tax men in order to obtain funds with which to compensate them for the loss of estates which they had no desire to lose? It was the intrinsic difficulty of any attempt to return nationalised property to its original owners which daunted Mary's Commons, and not any marked predilection for protestantism.

APPENDIX:
EXTRACTS FROM AUGMENTATION ACCOUNTS

(From the roll of the Treasurer of the court of Augmentations for the period from 24 April 1536, when the court was first established, to Michaelmas 1538. Public Record Office, E 323/1, Part I. A full transcript of the original would be far too voluminous to give here. In the version that follows the main items of receipt and expenditure are given to show the kind of information which the account contains. It should be observed that in setting out his figures the treasurer follows the older form of a 'charge and discharge' account, in which the accountant's object is not to present a credit and debit account in the modern manner, but simply to arrive at a statement of his own outstanding liability. It should also be borne in mind that even at the end of the period covered by this account the process of dissolving the larger abbeys had not gone very far. It should also be noted that the forfeited abbeys and the Lancashire houses were not handled by Augmentations, but by the Court of General Surveyors and the Duchy of Lancaster respectively. This account, therefore, covers mainly the dissolution of the lesser abbeys, and the amounts of money handled represent only a small proportion of the total proceeds of the dissolution. All the figures given below have been converted from Roman to Arabic numerals.)

The account of Thomas Pope, treasurer of the
Court of Augmentations

for the period from 24 April 28 Henry VIII
to Michaelmas 30 Henry VIII

Outstanding liabilities: NIL, because this is the first account since the creation of the court.

Received:
from the following, during the three years of account, 28, 29, & 30 Henry VIII:—

Geoffrey Chamber, receiver-general of purchased lands	£4785 : 0 : 3
John Freeman, receiver for Lincolnshire	£3661 : 10 : 0
John Danaster, receiver for Oxford, Bucks. and Berks.	£2058 : 0 : 0
Richard Paulet, receiver for Southants. Wilts. and Gloucs.	£1099 : 9 : 0
Francis Jobson, receiver for Essex, Herts. and Beds.	£1920 : 0 : 0

George Gifford, receiver for Northants. Warwick, Leics. and Rutland	£2688 : 12 : 2
John Scudamore, receiver for Hereford, Staffs. Salop. and Worcs.	£1665 : 6 : 2
Sir Thomas Arundell, receiver for Devon, Cornwall and Somerset	£1295 : 7 : 3½
Edward Waters, receiver for the dioceses of Llandaff and St. David's	£1165 : 8 : 2
Thomas Spilman, receiver for Middlesex, Kent and London	£1144 : 3 : 8⅝
William Blithman, receiver for the bishopric of Durham and the archdeaconry of Richmond	£420 : 0 : 0
William Green, receiver for Northumbs. Cumbs. and Westmorland	£173 : 6 : 8
William Bolles, receiver for Notts. Derbys. and Cheshire	£1275 : 0 : 0
John Morice, receiver for Surrey and Sussex	£1177 : 17 : 0
William Leigh, receiver for Cambs. and Hunts.	£753 : 14 : 9
Leonard Beckwith, receiver for Yorkshire	£1039 : 11 : 8¾
Richard Southwell, receiver for Norfolk and Suffolk	£1174 : 12 : 9
William Stump, receiver for the dioceses of St. Asaph and Bangor	£235 : 3 : 1½
TOTAL	£27732 : 2 : 9⅜

Also received from the following, from the sale of gold and silver plate from houses suppressed between 24 April 28 Henry VIII and 24 April 30 Henry VIII:—

John Freeman	£917 : 2 : 8
John Danaster	£984 : 16 : 5½
Richard Paulet	£587 : 14 : 1⅝
Thomas Spilman	£234 : 4 : 8
Francis Jobson	£277 : 7 : 10⅝
George Gifford	£882 : 16 : 8⅛
John Scudamore	£273 : 0 : 7
Sir Thomas Arundell	£578 : 13 : 2½
Richard Southwell	£357 : 19 : 6
Edward Waters	£447 : 8 : 5⅞
William Blithman	£347 : 14 : 8
William Bolles	£239 : 19 : 10
John Morice	£185 : 4 : 10¾
William Leigh	£164 : 5 : 1
Leonard Beckwith	£275 : 11 : 10⅜
William Stump	£41 : 13 : 9
William Green	£191 : 14 : 6¾
TOTAL	£6987 : 8 : 11⅛

Also received from the following religious houses, by way of fines for exemption from suppression:—

Bindon	Dorset	£300 : 0 : 0
St. James'	Northampton	£333 : 6 : 8
Delapre	Northampton	£266 : 13 : 4
St. Mary's nunnery	Winchester	£333 : 6 : 8
Huntingdon	Hunts.	£133 : 6 : 8
Biddlesden	Bucks.	£133 : 6 : 8
Shap	Westmorland	£266 : 13 : 4
Hull Charterhouse	Yorks.	£233 : 6 : 8
Kyme	Lincs.	£200 : 0 : 0
Stixwold	Lincs.	£21 : 13 : 4
Ulverscroft	Leics.	£166 : 13 : 4
Polsloe	Devon	£400 : 0 : 0
Cannonsleigh	Devon	£200 : 0 : 0
Newstead	Notts.	£233 : 6 : 8
Beauvale	Notts.	£166 : 13 : 4
Wallingwells	Notts.	£66 : 13 : 4
Neath	Glamorgan	£150 : 0 : 0
Whitland	St. David's	£400 : 0 : 0
Strata Florida	Carmarthen	£66 : 13 : 4
St. Mary's	Chester	£160 : 0 : 0
Dale	Derbys.	£166 : 13 : 4
Repton	Derbys.	£266 : 13 : 4
Wormsley	Hereford	£200 : 0 : 0
Lymbrook	Hereford	£53 : 6 : 8
Alnwick	Northumberland	£200 : 0 : 0
Lacock	Wilts.	£300 : 0 : 0
St. Thomas'	Stafford	£133 : 6 : 8
Croxden	Staffs.	£100 : 0 : 0
Rocester	Staffs.	£100 : 0 : 0
Hulton	Staffs.	£66 : 13 : 4
Bruisyard	Suffolk	£60 : 0 : 0
St. Anne's Coventry	Warwicks.	£20 : 0 : 0
Polesworth	Warwicks.	£50 : 0 : 0

	TOTAL	£5948 : 6 : 8
Also received: from the sale of lands	TOTAL	£29847 : 16 : 5
from fines for leases	TOTAL	£1006 : 17 : 0
from other sources	TOTAL	£95 : 4 : 4

TOTAL LIABILITY   £71616 : 16 : 1½

OF WHICH he is discharged for:—

Payment of fees and wages	£1675 : 14 : 0
Payment of annuities	£261 : 3 : 4
Payment of pensions	£448 : 18 : 4
Necessary costs of the court of Augmentations	£37 : 11 : 7
Necessary costs of the treasurer	£375 : 16 : 8
Necessary costs of messengers	£58 : 15 : 4
Purchase of Lands	£5702 : 1 : 11¾
Value of jewels surrendered to the King's use	£200 : 0 : 0
Payments ordered by the chancellor and council of the court of Augmentations (to surveyors and other officials)	£1416 : 6 : 8½
Payments by decree of the court of Augmentations (arrears of pensions, debts of monastic houses, etc.)	£2725 : 6 : 8½
Value of jewels passed to the master of the King's jewel house	£89 : 4 : 8
Value of vestments given into the keeping of Sir Anthony Denny (keeper of the privy purse)	£46 : 13 : 4
Value of ornaments given into keeping of Sir Richard Long	£10 : 0 : 0

Payments by warrant, comprising:—

administrative expenses	£40 : 0 : 0	
Purchase of lands	£900 : 0 : 0	
fencing Hampton Court	£600 : 0 : 0	
dissolution of Abingdon	£600 : 0 : 0	
victualling two ships, the *Sweepstake* and the *Lion*	£106 : 9 : 0	
building works at Westminster, Chelsea and Hackney	£2662 : 0 : 1	
unspecified expenses	£2400 : 5 : 6	
to Sir Richard Cotton, treasurer of Prince Edward's household	£5000 : 0 : 0	
for fencing Hartwell Park	£210 : 0 : 0	
for building a ship	£1000 : 0 : 0	
repairing Westminster Hall	£1000 : 0 : 0	
fencing the new park at Canterbury	£100 : 0 : 0	
TOTAL	£14618 : 14 : 7	£14618 : 14 : 7

Sums paid into the King's coffers:—

per John Gostwick	£11247 : 14 : 11¼
per Thomas Heneage	£2666 : 13 : 4
per Thomas Heneage and Anthony Denny	£6666 : 13 : 4
TOTAL	£20581 : 1 : 7¼ £20581 : 1 : 7¼

SUM OF ALL EXPENSES ALLOWED AND PAYMENTS MADE		£48247 : 8 : 10
BALANCE OUTSTANDING		£23369 : 7 : 3½

Further allowances

for supposed silver gilt, found to be copper gilt	£3 : 0 : 8	
for base matter included in the weight of jewels	£15 : 12 : 1	
for plate found to be short weight	£2 : 0 : 5	
fee for audit of account	£40 : 0 : 0	
BALANCE OUTSTANDING		£23308 : 14 : 1½
Arrears due from purchasers of lands		£15006 : 13 : 5
PERSONAL LIABILITY OF ACCOUNTANT		£8302 : 0 : 8½

10

The Fate of the Religious

ANY account of the lives and careers of the ex-religious in the years following the suppression of the monastic orders should begin with a word of caution. Although we do possess in contemporary records an abundance of references to individual monks and nuns, and can follow up quite a number of careers in some detail, we remain almost totally ignorant of the lives of the great majority, and have no sure means of knowing how representative of the whole body of more than 9,000 ex-religious is the comparatively restricted number of cases available for us to study. Unlike a modern statistician we cannot select our own well-balanced sample. It is chosen for us by the chance of being preserved in the surviving records of the law courts, the probate registries and the church, and, for this reason, it may be unduly weighted in favour of the more fortunate of the dispossessed monks and nuns.

The Nature of the Evidence

Legal records are the least likely to be weighted in this way, for most of the ex-religious who appeared in court (with the exception of the quite considerable number who, in the reign of Mary, got into trouble with the ecclesiastical authorities because they had married) did so as witnesses, in which capacity their integrity was of more significance than their wealth. The probate registries, on the other hand, provide us principally with the names of those who were sufficiently well off to have property worth bequeathing, and only the more fortunate who secured promotion in the church are noted in the record of institutions to benefices. And so when our examples are drawn from records of these last two types we must always be on our guard against too readily assuming that our sample is necessarily typical of the whole. The most that we can say by way of general judgment is that among the ex-religious whose careers are known to us there seem to have been very few cases of genuine difficulty or hardship. We cannot legitimately go further and claim that all the rest must surely have fared as well as the sample few.

We must next distinguish clearly between two main categories of ex-religious, the pensioned and the pensionless. The first group was almost certainly considerably the larger. It included all the abbots, priors and prioresses from the small houses dissolved in 1536, all the inhabitants of those small houses which were not suppressed in 1536 but were allowed to survive until 1538 or 1539, and all the monks and nuns from the larger houses which surrendered from November 1537 onwards, including in this last group all those who in 1536 had chosen to transfer to such houses from smaller ones which were suppressed. Thus, of all the monks, canons and nuns, the only ones who did not get pensions were those who had rejected the chance to transfer to larger houses in 1536 and had chosen to take capacities instead. But to these must be added all the friars, and the combined total of ex-religious without pensions becomes quite considerable.

The Pensionless: Monks and Friars

The names of nearly 850 monks and canons and of over 1,000 friars who obtained capacities in the years 1536–40 are entered in a register of dispensations kept by the archbishop of Canterbury at Lambeth.[1] Of these only thirty-four had pensions, and only forty-eight of those without pensions have been found enjoying livings in the church at any later date. Thus a minimum of around 1,800 regular clergy were, in the years of the dissolution, turned out of their former homes to face the future with 'no visible means of support'. What they did, or how they fared, we do not at present know, but we must not be too eager to jump to the conclusion that they were all reduced to beggary. Indeed in the case of the ex-monks and ex-canons this seems very unlikely. They had none of them been obliged to take capacities or to embark upon new careers. The alternative of transfer to a surviving house had in every case been open to them, and those who had knowingly rejected the security of life in a larger abbey had surely

[1] For the contents and importance of this register (now published as *Faculty Office Registers* 1534–49 ed. D. S. Chambers, Clarendon Press, 1966) see the article by G. E. J. Hodgett in the *Journal of Ecclesiastical History*, vol. XIII, 1962.

done so with some alternative career in mind. There were, after all, openings for them as chantry or stipendiary priests, as chaplains or tutors in private houses, as clerk in administration or business, and those who found such employment might easily live out their lives without leaving any trace of their names in the records.

Similar post-dissolution careers were also open to the ex-friars, and some of them did very well for themselves, notably the former Dominican, John Scory, who was bishop of Rochester and Chichester in succession in Edward's reign, and was appointed to Hereford by Elizabeth, or John Hilsey, another Dominican, who succeeded John Fisher at Rochester. But on the whole the ex-friars had a rather harder time than the pensionless ex-monks and canons, for when they surrendered their friaries they had no option but to accept capacities and a small gratuity at the hands of the suppressors. No pensions were awarded, no chance of transfer to another house was offered. The friars had always lived on charity. There was no need therefore, in the eyes of the government, to compensate them for the loss of a secure living, for such they had never enjoyed. Let them now seek honest labour or rely on the good will of their neighbours and friends. In the latter case their last state would be no worse than their first. The friars thus form the largest group of ex-religious persons about whose fate and fortune after the dissolution we really know very little indeed.

The Pensionless: Nuns

The fate of the nuns who chose capacities in 1536 is equally obscure. As we saw in Chapter 5 above, the prospects for a woman of employment outside the cloister were very slender, and in fact very few nuns did not choose to be transferred to surviving houses of their own order. The few who did go out into the world in 1536 are exceedingly difficult to trace. Only very occasionally do we catch glimpses of their later careers. The best documented life history is that of Margaret Basfurth, one of the nuns from the little house of Moxby which lay about nine miles to the north of York city. In 1554, when she was brought before the archbishop's court and charged with having violated her nuns' vows by marrying a certain Roger Newstead, this is the account she gave of herself:

'About fourteen years of age she was professed nun in the said monastery and there continued to she was twenty years of age, at what time she went out of the said monastery, the house being dissolved, she having no pension appointed nor other living toward her finding, and so continued unmarried to about a thirteen years after and then for lack of living she married.'

Moxby was dissolved in 1536, so that Margaret would appear to have married in 1549 at the age of thirty-three. In the previous year there had passed through parliament an act permitting the clergy to marry (2 & 3 Edward VI, c. 21), a statute which Margaret seems to have regarded as releasing her also from her obligation to celibacy since her marriage followed so soon after. But in Mary's reign this statute was repealed and proceedings were taken in the ecclesiastical courts against the married clergy and married nuns. Margaret was obliged to separate from her husband and was forbidden by order of the court to associate with him in future save publicly in church and market, though even then she was not to speak to him unless there were at least three or four other persons present. She was also required to resume her nuns' habit, though her original capacity was confirmed by the grant of a licence

'that she may continue and remain in any honest place without the said house of Moxby'.

And so once again this ex-nun found herself 'without living' for the court made no provision for her maintenance.

Margaret's story ends, however, on a happier note. In 1586 we come across her once again, now over seventy years of age, but once more known and accepted as the wife of Roger Newstead from whom she had been separated more than thirty years earlier. The chief question raised by this nun's account of her own career is how she managed to live during those thirteen years between the dissolution of Moxby and her marriage, when she had 'no pension appointed nor other living'. Did she have to rely upon the charity of her relatives, as apparently did Joan Redman 'late nun of Nunmonkton' who found a home with her married sister Elizabeth Lyndley, and was remembered in the will of Elizabeth's father-in-law in 1541? Did she find employment as governess or companion in the household of some lady of rank? And what did she mean when she said that 'then for lack of living she married'? Had the death of some near relative, or the loss of some employment reduced her to such straits that marriage was the only road to survival? And what did she do for a living between the day of her divorce from Roger Newstead in

Mary's reign and her reunion with him in Elizabeth's? These are some of the gaps in her story that we should like to see filled.

And yet, for all these unanswered questions, we still know far more about Margaret Basfurth than we do about any of the other nuns who went out of their cloisters unpensioned in 1536. Much more typical of the fragmentary nature of our knowledge of the lives of such ex-religious is the evidence relating to one of Margaret's former fellow nuns, Elizabeth Burnett. They both appeared as witnesses in the same tithe case which in 1586 showed us a last glimpse of Margaret reunited with her husband Roger, but all we learn about Elizabeth is that she is still a spinster and 'worth forty shillings and more'. We get no clue to the nature of the life she has been leading since she and Margaret left Moxby full half a century earlier. Her name does not appear on the pension list of any neighbouring house. It is almost certain therefore that she took her capacity in 1536 and faced the secular world at the same time as Margaret, and as ill provided for financially. How had she managed to stay single and survive despite her 'lack of living'? Any answer to such a question must be at best a straightforward guess.

The pensionless religious thus formed a not insignificant proportion of the total number, and, because of the paucity of the evidence relating to their later careers we are unable to assert with any degree of confidence that the dissolution did not bring for them substantial physical as well as spiritual hardship in its train. Yet, on the other hand, we have just as little right to assume that none of them found their feet and carved out for themselves quite comfortable careers. The truth, which we shall probably never know for certain, lies somewhere in between.

The Pensioners

When we turn from the pensionless to the pensioned we find ourselves on slightly firmer ground. We do at least know the size of their pensions. There was no national uniform standard for these and they varied from house to house. The widest variations are to be found in the amounts awarded to abbots and other heads of houses, whose pensions are, generally speaking, proportionate to the value of the property which they surrendered. The richer the house, the greater the abbot's pension, so that the abbot of Fountains, which was rated by the Tenths commissioners at over £1,000, got £100 a year, the abbot of Whitby, valued at £419, had £66 13s. 4d., the prioress of Nunmonkton, worth £75, was awarded £13 6s. 8d., but the prioress of Nunburnholme, taxed at only £6, had to be content with £3 6s. 8d. There was some rough justice about this. The pensions were awarded and accepted as compensation for the loss by the abbot of his living and status in society when his house was dissolved. The heads of the larger houses had been accustomed for many years to living like great lords (the abbot of York wore fine silks and rode a richly-caparisoned horse; the abbot of Roche was accustomed to hunting and hawking parties on his outlying manors) and so had a right to lordly pensions. The heads of humbler houses had never known such luxury and should not expect to enjoy it now.

The variations in the amount of the pensions awarded to the 'rank and file' of the religious are very much less remarkable, though the size of individual awards is still determined to a certain extent by the wealth and size of the houses concerned, for it was not to be expected that the crown would more than occasionally, and in extreme cases such as those tabled on p. 123 above, commit itself to paying out more in pensions than it expected to get in rents. Why, after all, should the ex-religious be given pensions larger than their proportional share in the revenues of their former house? As a general rule, then, the larger the abbey the more generous were the pensions awarded to its former inhabitants. But within each community we also find variations in pension rates. Some two or three of the more senior monks or nuns, those who held positions of responsibility, sub-priors, bursars, cellarers and the like, received slightly larger sums. Very junior monks and novices who had not yet taken their vows often received rather less than the majority of their brethren.

Typical of the pension lists for the larger abbeys is that of Selby, valued at £739, where the abbot got £100, the prior £8, five senior monks £6 each, six others £5 6s. 8d. each, nine junior monks £5 each and two novices £2 13s. 4d. apiece. This should, however, be contrasted with the pension list for a small nunnery, such as Hampole, where, in addition to the prioress who got £10 and the sub-prioress who was awarded £3 6s. 8d., there were five senior nuns with £2 13s. 4d. each, four others with £2 6s. 8d. each and eight juniors with only £2 each. The average pension at Selby, not counting the abbot and the two novices, was almost £5 10s. 0d. The average at Hampole, excluding the prioress, was exactly £2 6s. 8d. These local averages are in fact very close to the average figures for the whole country.

The Real Value of the Pensions

So much for the figures, but what do they mean? How comfortable a living did these pensions provide? The critical figure is £5 a year which can be taken to be the usual minimum for a fully professed monk in priest's orders. The men who received less than this amount were usually novices or very junior monks not long committed to the regular life who could be expected to adapt themselves to changed circumstances more easily than their seniors. Was £5 a year in 1540 a mere pittance or a modest competence? A glance through the pages of the *Valor Ecclesiasticus*, that great survey of clerical incomes compiled by the Tenths commissioners in 1535, reveals a number of very poor benefices where the incumbent was expected to live on little more than £4 a year. We also know from the records of the dissolution that the resident chaplains in some of the smaller nunneries were paid as little as £2 a year over and above their keep. This last was reckoned by the suppression commissioners to be worth £2 13s. 4d. a year, so that the total value of such a chaplaincy, and of the pension given to the chaplain by way of compensation after the dissolution, was £4 13s. 4d. a year. But vicarages rated at £4 a year were exceptionally poor livings in 1535, and the figure of £8, which is the lowest value of benefice to which the pluralities act of 1529 was to apply, would be a better one to take to represent the level of a modest competency at that date. By these standards a pension of £5 a year granted in 1538 or 1539 should not be regarded as much more than a subsistence allowance for a priest. Indeed there is evidence to show that in 1538 £5 6s. 8d. a year was considered by some to be too small a stipend to attract a prospective curate.

We must also remember that the closing decades of the reign of Henry VIII saw the great tide of sixteenth-century inflation flowing, and that, in a period of inflation, it is always the pensioner with his fixed income who fares worst. The incumbency which was valued at £4 in 1535 might well have come to be worth much more by 1545, especially if the parson still farmed his own glebe and collected his tithes in kind. The recipient of a £5 pension, however, received no cost of living bonus in later years, and found the purchasing power of his few pounds steadily waning away.

Taxation and Arrears

A £5 pension was, therefore, far from being a fortune. And yet the sum awarded was not the sum the pensioner received. There were nearly always deductions to be made from the gross sum before the balance was paid out. In the first place the Augmentations receiver, or other official through whose hands the money passed, was entitled to deduct his fee. Early in the reign of Edward VI this was fixed by statute at the rate of 4*d*. for every £1 of pension, with an additional 4*d*. for making out the necessary receipt form if the pensioner did not supply his own. The fact that parliament in the same act prescribed penalties to be imposed upon those who levied fees in excess of the stipulated maxima suggests strongly that some officials in previous years had not been content with deductions as modest as these. Together with his fee the receiver also deducted the amount of the current clerical subsidy. In most years this tax ran at the rate of 2*s*. in the £1 on all pensions, though in 1545 and 1546 the cost of the war forced the rate up to 3*s*. And so we find that in an average year the monk with a £5 pension received in fact no more than £4 7*s*. 8*d*. (£5 gross, less 10*s*. subsidy, 1*s*. 8*d*. receiver's fee and 8*d*. for the two half-yearly receipts), and in the war years only £4 2*s*. 8*d*. (subsidy 15*s*., other deductions as before). Other rates of pension were similarly taxed, and those with more than £20 a year suffered during the war years an additional and substantial deduction of one-quarter of the gross value by way of a 'benevolence'. Only the poorer nuns received any general tax relief when from 1545 onwards those whose pension rate was £2 a year or less were exempted from paying the subsidy.

But taxation and fee deductions were not the only financial burdens which the ex-religious had to bear. Another, and perhaps more serious cause of hardship was the delay in the payment of pensions which arose, partly through negligence on the part of the paying authorities, but mainly because of the financial embarrassment of the government in the reign of Edward VI. So bad did the situation then become that a nationwide survey of pensioners was taken in 1552–3 which revealed that many pensions were a year in arrears, some eighteen months, and a few as much as two years or more. Such delays could occasion great hardship to those whose pensions were their only source of income.

These Edwardian pension returns also reveal that some of the ex-religious had sold their pension rights, preferring the certainty of a few pounds cash in hand to the uncertainty of future payments, or perhaps obliged by pressing penury to sell their rights to someone who could afford to wait for the arrears to be paid off. There was nothing illegal about such sales. As long as the purchaser was able to prove to the satisfaction of the Augmentations officials that the original pensioner was still alive he could continue to draw the regular half-yearly instalments. For both the vendor and the purchaser such sales were of course speculations upon the life of the pensioner, and the terms of the bargain would have varied widely according to the age and state of health of the latter. Few details of such sales survive. One former monk of Meaux, Martin Wren, sold his pension of £6 at the age of 46 to a citizen of York for £20 4s. 0d. As Wren lived on for at least another seven years the purchaser in this case secured a good bargain, and eventually recouped more than twice his purchase money. Wren could, however, afford to capitalise his pension thus, for he had by then secured a vicarage. The purchaser of the pension of Elizabeth Clyfton of Swine got an even better bargain. Aged 27 in 1539 when her house was dissolved, she sold her pension sometime between then and 1552, and was still alive in 1573, so the purchaser would have enjoyed over twenty years return upon his outlay. How Elizabeth lived after selling her pension, or even what price she got for it, we just do not know.

Opportunities in the Church

Taxation, fees and arrears combined to make life difficult for the ex-monk who had only his pension to live on. But, of course, the fact that he had a pension did not prevent him from seeking means to supplement it, and many an ex-religious very rapidly found himself absorbed into the parochial structure of the church. Indeed the very terms upon which monastic pensions were granted were calculated to encourage such a development, for they were to be paid for term of life or until such time as the recipient should be promoted by the king to one or more benefices equal to or greater in value than the amount of his pension. Thus every time an ex-monk was nominated to a living in the gift of the crown there was one less pension to pay, and so it is not surprising to find the religious benefiting extensively from royal patronage. On the other hand a monk who could secure a benefice from the hand of a private patron was able to keep his pension as well, and this fact would tend to encourage the religious to seek such patrons before the king could make provision for them.

Of course the supply of church livings was limited, and far from sufficient to absorb all the ex-monks at once. Some had to wait for many years before their turn came. Others, thanks to the foresight of their abbots and brethren before the dissolution, secured a living almost as soon as they left the cloister. Nearly all the above points are illustrated in the post-suppression history of the rectory of Wilby in Norfolk. Before the dissolution this living was in the gift of the abbots of St. Mary's York. Some time, shortly before the surrender of his house in 1539, the last abbot assigned the right of making the next presentation to a man who could be relied upon to look to the interests of the monks. And so, when the living next fell vacant in 1540, it was Guy Kelsaye, lately prior of St. Mary's, who was nominated to the rectory. Kelsaye already had his pension of £13 6s. 8d. a year which, because his promotion had come from a private patron, he continued to enjoy in addition to the proceeds of his rectory which was valued in 1535 at £7 4s. 7½d.

After Kelsaye's appointment, however, the right of presentation reverted to the abbey, represented now by its new proprietor, the king. And so when, in 1553, Kelsaye, now an old man, resigned his cure, it was the crown which nominated his successor. Even so this proved to be another, though much junior, ex-monk of St. Mary's, Thomas Pierson. Hitherto he had enjoyed a pension of £5 a year, but now, because he owed his new promotion to the king, that was stopped and he was left with the rectory alone. The contrast between the two cases, Kelsaye securing a living within a year of leaving his abbey, and yet continuing to draw his pension, and Pierson waiting fourteen years for his promotion and then losing his pension, is very marked, and demonstrates effectively how varied could be the fortunes of two ex-monks from the same house, even when they both in turn served the same parish.

Of course many ex-monks fared even better than Guy Kelsaye. Most fortunate were those whose abbeys were already cathedral churches, or were 'refounded' as such by Henry VIII, and who found themselves retained on the staff of the new foundation. Not all the monks from these great abbeys eventually became canons of the new cathedrals. Even at the ancient cathedral priories such as Norwich,

Durham, Worcester or Canterbury, only about half the monks were allowed to remain, and the rest were pensioned. However, the abbot of Peterborough became the first bishop of that see, the abbot of Thame became first bishop of Oxford, and the abbot of Tewkesbury was transferred to Gloucester as first bishop there. At Chester, though the first bishop was an ex-friar, the first dean was the former prior of the abbey.

At all levels, from bishop to chantry priest, we find the ex-religious playing their part in the life of the church. Indeed the very number of ex-regulars who were available to fill vacancies as they arose had quite a depressive effect upon the rate of entry to the priesthood. From the late 1530s onwards there was an abrupt and serious decline in the number of men coming forward for ordination. This may, of course, have been due in part to the general uncertainty of the times, and to the understandable reluctance of young men to embark upon clerical careers when the very future of the church seemed so much in doubt. It may also have been due in part to the progressive whittling away of clerical privileges so that there was no longer any very good reason why men who had no real vocation to the priesthood should take orders simply in order to enjoy the legal privileges attaching to clerical status. But, even allowing for the operation of such factors as these, the turning loose upon the clerical employment market of so many qualified priests in so short a space of time must have made a considerable contribution to this falling off in the rate of ordinations.

Secular Opportunities

Though a career in the church was the obvious one for an ex-monk to follow, it is clear that there were some who profited from the dissolution to develop talents of a more secular kind. Such a one was Thomas Pepper. Dismissed from his abbey, Kirkstall, in 1539 with an annual pension of £5, he managed in the fifteen years between then and his death to acquire a considerable amount of property. His will, dated 27 March 1553, which is given in full in the appendix to this chapter, includes cash bequests which add up to more than £86 besides ten angels of gold and a debt of £20 which he generously forgave the debtor. In addition he made provision for the disposal of various leaseholds which must have been worth very considerably more to him than the £20 or so he paid annually in rents. Perhaps the most valuable of his properties was the ironworks at Weetwood from

L

the tenants of which he was accustomed to receive two shillings for every bloom produced. Besides these fixed assets Pepper also possessed a considerable quantity of grain and livestock which he bequeathed in detail, together with a long list of household and personal goods. At least two menservants, and possibly three women servants as well, are mentioned in his will which shows him to have been living in a style and manner more appropriate to a minor gentleman than to an ex-religious with a subsistence pension.

At the time of the dissolution Pepper was one of the junior monks at Kirkstall. Ordained accolyte in 1533, and raised to the priesthood as late as 1534, his name stood 25th on a pension list of thirty-one. His pension rate of £5 was shared by five other juniors. Only the two novices got less than this. How then did Pepper manage to acquire before his death so substantial a share of this world's goods? It is probable, though not certain, that he supplemented his pension by serving as rector of Adel, a living valued in 1535 at just over £16 a year. He also inherited some of his properties, chiefly a dwelling house in Bramley, from his father, John Pepper yeoman, who died in 1548. But the more valuable of Thomas Pepper's holdings seem to have been acquired by purchase. We know, for example, that the Weetwood ironworks were leased to Sir Robert Neville by the abbot and convent of Kirkstall some sixteen months before the dissolution of their house, and that, though he later had to fend off a counter claim to the property, Sir Robert died in possession in 1542 and left the remaining years of his lease to his widow. How, or on what terms, it passed from her to Pepper we cannot say, but it seems most unlikely that he received it as a gift. To have prospered as he did on so small a pension and so modest a patrimony, Thomas Pepper must indeed have been a man with gifts more suited to the counting house than to the cloister.

The Evidence of Wills

The last wills and testaments of quite a number of Pepper's former brethren have also been preserved, and reveal that among the monks from Kirkstall such prosperity as he attained was quite exceptional. More typical was the fortune of Edward Heptonstall, one of the senior monks, whose pension was £6 13s. 4d. and who died in 1558. With ten nieces and nephews to remember, besides friends and neighbours, his individual cash bequests were very modest indeed, and add up to no more than £3 12*s.* 0*d.* in all. No real estate is mentioned in his will, his chief treasures were a pair of virginals, a vestment of silver and damask velvet and a chest full of books from the abbey library. These last he hopefully instructed his executors to return to Kirkstall if the abbey should be refounded in their lifetime. If it was not, then they were to pass on the books to their executors 'to deliver them with like intent'. Alas for Heptonstall's hopes, only a handful of books from the former library of Kirkstall now remain, and it is very doubtful whether any of these is from his personal collection.

Heptonstall's will thus shows us him living out his days in simple comfort surrounded by his books and music, and dreaming of a return to the cloister, not well-to-do like Pepper, but certainly more fortunate than yet a third ex-monk of Kirkstall, Gabriel Lofthouse. This latter, one of the seniors in 1539, ordained priest in 1522, and therefore probably well into his fifties when he died in 1552, secured a chaplaincy at Richmond to supplement his £6 pension. And yet his will reveals the paucity of his possessions. Apart from his bedding, which went to his brother, he had nothing to leave but a shirt, a long gown, a wooden spoon tipped with silver and a little over one guinea in cash.

Three wills; three monks from the same house; three very different fortunes. There is nothing exceptional or unexpected about this. Some, like Pepper, very successfully adapted themselves to changed circumstances; some, like Heptonstall, managed to maintain a reasonable standard of living though they never quite came to terms with the secular world; others, like Lofthouse, fell on hard times. But despite their varied fortunes the monks of Kirkstall did not altogether forget that they had once shared a common life. Many of them continued to live in the vicinity of their former home, in Leeds, Adel, Horsforth and Bramley, and kept in touch with one another. When they made their wills their former brethren were seldom far from their minds. Thomas Bartlett, who died in Leeds in 1542, left to Thomas Elles his best gown and a silver cup, and passed on 'to the adornment of the high altar at Leeds' his portion of 'a suit of vestments' which he had shared with yet another ex-monk, the late John Harrison. A few years later another ex-monk of Kirkstall dwelling in Leeds, Richard Elles, remembered on his deathbed his former brother Anthony Jackson in nearby Horsforth, called on him to witness his will and left him a gown, a brooch, a horse, a vestment, an altar cloth and other linen. In 1553 this same Anthony was one of the beneficiaries named in Thomas Pepper's will, along with Leonard Wyndresse the former sub-prior, William Lupton and Richard Wood. Such a keeping up of old ties between fellow members of the same community is by no means unusual. Many examples of the same sort of thing can be found in other parts of the country, and others besides Heptonstall hoped to see their houses rise again. Few, however, were prepared to do more than wait and hope.

Communities which Continued

Quite exceptional was the attempt made by some of the monks of Monk Bretton, near Barnsley, to continue to live together after the dissolution, and to practise their former discipline. Though they had surrendered to the king their priory and its property, and had received in return capacities and pensions, they had not been debarred by any statute from attempting to continue to the best of their ability to follow the rules of their order. Immediately after the surrender William Browne, the prior, took a house in nearby Worsborough and retired thither in company with Thomas Frobisher the sub-prior, and two monks, Thomas Wilkinson and Richard Hinchcliffe. With them they took nearly 150 of the books from the priory library together with the recently compiled chartulary, or register of the priory's title deeds, and it is clear that their intention was to continue the common life to which they were accustomed. Their determination to preserve as much as possible of their library was in keeping with the care that they had been wont to bestow upon their books in the days before the dissolution. In the last decade of the life of their house many of their books had been rebound and furnished with clasps made from the metal of an unwanted mazer, and a team of monks had been employed in copying all the priory deeds into the new-made chartulary

'lest any casualty should happen to the originals by fire'.

This work was also 'bound into a book' by one of the monks, and furnished with a metal clasp. It survives today, though not in its original binding, and it is from notes written on leaves inserted in it that we learn the story of Browne and his companions.

All the books they saved had to be purchased from the suppressors, for the library was legally part of the property of the priory and passed to the crown at its surrender. What price they paid, or where they found the money to pay it, we do not know. Prior Browne, who had a gratuity of £75 and an annual pension of £40, was best able to afford the purchase money, but in fact bought no more than thirty-one books. The biggest purchase was, somewhat surprisingly, made by the most junior of the four monks, Richard Hinchcliffe, who

'acquired at his own expense and by his own hand'

no less than seventy-three works, though his gratuity was only 53s. 4d. and his pension £5 6s. 8d.

Most of the books which these monks bought and took to Worsborough with them were biblical commentaries or devotional manuals whose titles convey little or nothing to the modern reader. Some, however, are worth noting. A *Musica Monachorum* by John Norton, prior of the Carthusian house of Mount Grace less than a decade before its dissolution, the *Colloquia* of Erasmus, his translation of the New Testament, and a tract by John Ditemberg defending monastic vows against the attacks of Luther all indicate by their presence the determination of the monks to keep their library up to date. Similarly a handbook for novices compiled by one of the monks concerned in the purchase, and copies of medical works in the hand of another, are evidence of the literary abilities and intellectual interests of this little group.

The combined pensions of Browne and his three companions amounted to more than £58, so that if they pooled their resources, as very probably they did, they should have been able to maintain a fairly comfortable standard of living. All four were still alive in 1552, but by 1558, twenty years after the surrender of their house, death had begun to break up the little community. Frobisher, the subprior, had gone, but even at his departing had borne witness to his sense of unity with his fellows by bequeathing to them his share of the monastic library. The lead he then gave was followed by the prior himself who, at his death a few years later, left to his surviving companions the all-important chartulary and his portion of the books. The death of the prior removed the main prop of the little community, and deprived them of the support of his more generous pension. The two survivors had now less than £12 between them.

In any case it is unlikely that Wilkinson survived the prior by many years. By 1568 he too was dead, and Hinchcliffe, the sole survivor and now possessor of all the books, had moved to Handsworth, near Sheffield, where he was perhaps rector. Less than four years later, however, he had returned to Worsborough to die in the house of Mr. Francis Wortley, to whom he left the precious chartulary. Thirty-six years after its formal surrender the community of Monk Bretton was at last extinct.

A somewhat similar attempt to keep the common life alive was made by the prioress and four nuns from Kirklees, a small nunnery in the Calder valley. After the dissolution of their house they continued to live together for many years in a house in nearby Mirfield. They were by no means as well off as the monks from Monk Bretton, for their combined pensions cannot have come to more than £9, unless Isabel Saltonstall who had a corrody of 50s. as well as a pension, was one of their number. Even then they would have had no more than £11 10s. 0d. between the five of them. Joan Kyppax the prioress died in 1562 at the age of 75 or 76, and her death in all likelihood broke up the community. If Isabel Saltonstall had ever been a member of it she was so no longer when, in 1577, an unseemly slanging match with a neighbour led to her appearance in the bishop's court to face charges of defamation. At that date she was living near Halifax and, though known locally as 'the nun', had acquired a bad reputation as a scold.

The only other well-authenticated instance of members of a dissolved community continuing to live together is provided by the Cambridgeshire nunnery of Denney whose abbess, Elizabeth Throckmorton, took two or three of her sisters to live with her at her family home in Warwickshire.

Such attempts to keep the old community together are chiefly notable for their rarity. The great majority of the former religious seem to have been content to accept their fate and to adjust themselves to their new circumstances without a backward glance. The religious orders ceased to exist and their former members were absorbed into secular society with the minimum of disturbance.

The Plight of the Nuns

And yet readjustment for some must have been a difficult process, particularly for the nuns. The monks, whose pensions were as a general rule just about adequate to support them in somewhat spartan comfort, and who could hope for employment in various capacities both within and outside the church, had on the whole less cause for complaint than had the many nuns whose pensions were too small to give them financial independence and who had no ready way of supplementing their income from other sources. Some, of course, married, but, like Margaret Basfurth the pensionless nun whose career we noticed earlier (above, pp. 141–2), they had to wait until after the death of Henry VIII before they could do so legally. Then their pensions, small though they were, could take the place of the more usual dowry. But in Mary's reign all such marriages were dissolved, and we do not know how many ex-nuns, then separated from their husbands, were reunited with them when Elizabeth became queen.

Other nuns returned to their families with their pensions to help defray the cost of their keep. One such was Agnes Aunger from Nunappleton, who found a home with her brother-in-law Henry Burton of Bardsey, until his death in 1558. Thereafter his executors were charged with the duty of providing her with

'sufficient meat and drink and cloth during her life if she do suffer them to receive and have her pension'.

Another who returned home was Isabel Craik from Wilberfoss. In 1538, when she was still in her convent, her father died. In his will, drawn up shortly before his death, he made no mention of Isabel at all, evidently regarding her as sufficiently well provided for in the cloister. He had, after all, eight other sons and daughters to remember. Ten years later, when Isabel had been retired from the cloister on a pension of £1 6s. 8d., her mother died. This time Isabel was remembered in the will along with all the rest of the family, and received a considerable quantity of furnishings, some clothing, and an annuity of £3 6s. 8d. for life.

Wills, which provide so good an idea of the degree of comfort enjoyed by many an ex-monk in his years of retirement, are not so frequently found for nuns. This is in itself significant and suggests that few of them died possessed of property worth bequeathing. Furthermore, most of the surviving nuns' wills are those of abbesses and prioresses who, with their more substantial pensions, might be expected to have possessions worth disposing of in detail. Yet even between one prioress and another great discrepancies in wealth are sometimes revealed. Elizabeth Lord, last prioress of Wilberfoss, had only £8 a year by way of pension, but came of a prosperous family, being sister-in-law to George Gale, goldsmith and twice Lord Mayor of York. Consequently it is not surprising to find her able to make bequests in cash totalling nearly £70, besides several valuable pieces of plate, a dozen gold coins and an extensive wardrobe which included at least one gown of the latest London fashion. At the other end of the scale is Joan Harkay, last prioress of Ellerton in Swaledale to whom the suppression commissioners awarded the meagre pension of only £3 a year.[2] Apart from her bed, a gold ring, a silver spoon and twenty shillings in cash, she had little to leave when she died in 1550, but a limited collection of kitchenware, a single chair and two small chests containing her modest wardrobe. The total value of all her worldly possessions, including the ready money, was only £3 12s. 4d. Poor though she was, however, she did not forget her former sisters. To four of them she left one shilling each.

These four had all transferred to other houses when Ellerton had been suppressed in 1536, and had subsequently received modest pensions when their new homes had been dissolved some three years later. One of them, Agnes Aslayby, had married a priest, only to be separated from him in Mary's reign, but how or where the other three had lived after leaving the cloister we cannot tell. The fact that their former prioress named only four of her six former subordinates in her will may mean that they were the only ones who had kept in touch with her, or perhaps that they were living with or near her and trying to preserve some semblance of their former common life, though in view of Agnes Aslayby's marriage this does not seem very likely. It may, on the other hand, mean no more than that they were the only four known to Joan Harkay to be still alive at the time that she made her will. Such uncertainty is typical of the state of our knowledge of the after-careers of most of the rank and file of the nuns. We know, from the returns of the Edwardian pension commissioners that about half of all the pensioned nuns were still alive some fourteen years after the dissolution, but about fewer than one in ten of the survivors do we know any more than the bare fact of their survival.

We must therefore end this chapter as we began, by emphasising

[2] For the text of her will see the appendix to this chapter.

once again that the number of ex-religious upon whose post-dissolution lives we can throw any really positive light is relatively very small, and that in this sample of after-careers which has been selected for us by events beyond our control a disproportionate weight is given to the monks, and to the pensioners. Of the pensionless we know next to nothing, and about the nuns very little. We must be careful therefore not to assume, on the basis of an impressive number of well-attested cases of monkish prosperity, that all the ex-religious fared equally well, and that the dissolution left no hardship in its wake. On the other hand, cases in which there is much evidence of any real love of the religious life or of any attempt by members of a dissolved community to hold it together and to preserve the common life are significantly rare. Nor, in Mary's reign, when a few religious houses were re-founded by the queen, is there much evidence of any great rush to return to the cloister. With the notable exception of the Carthusians, the Bridgettines and the Observant Franciscans who so boldly resisted the establishment of the royal supremacy and suffered savage persecution for their pains, and who counted in their ranks some real devotees who attempted to revive their communities in exile, there seems, in the sixteenth century, to have been little real enthusiasm in England and Wales for the monastic ideal. Monasticism was an established and accepted institution, but few who entered the orders can have done so with any very vital sense of calling. When the end came they seemed for the most part well content to come to terms with the new order and to adapt themselves fairly readily to the ways of the world outside the cloister.

APPENDIX: MONASTIC WILLS

1. THE WILL OF THOMAS PEPPER, MONK OF KIRKSTALL

(From the Register of Archbishops Holgate and Heath of York, fol. 107. The spelling of the English text has been modernised and punctuation supplied. Amounts given in figures have been converted from Roman to Arabic numerals. Persons marked * can be identified as former monks of Kirkstall. For commentary see above, pp. 149–50.)

Testamentum Thome Pepper Clerke defuncti

In the Name of God, Amen. I, Sir Thomas Pepper of Adel in the county of York, sick in body and of perfect remembrance, do make my last will and testament the 27th day of March in the year of our

Lord God a thousand five hundred fifty and three in manner and form following:—FIRST bequeath my soul to the mercy of Almighty God the Holy and Most Blessed Trinity, and my body to be buried in the churchyard of Adel aforesaid, as I have appointed with Sir Anthony Jackson* my godfather. Also I bequeath all my goods both movable and immovable to my executors upon condition that my said executors shall give dispose and deliver the same according to the purport tenor and effect of this my present will in manner and form as hereafter appeareth, that is to say I bequeath to Nicholas Pepper my cousin 100 marks and all the years to come and unspent of my lease which I have of the abbey field sheep close and deeding for the farm paying, except that my farmers of Weetwood Smithies shall have liberty to mow and make in hay four loads in the said deeding at their own costs and charges with liberty to carry the same away and to pay no more for the same yearly during the said lease. Also I bequeath unto the said Nicholas the dwelling house of mine in Bramley and such other ground as is not in lease to Thomas Wroose of Bramley, and my lease of the same, and, after the expiration of the said lease, all the said tenements, paying the rent; and my part of the Styfield upon condition that he shall not set it nor let it to any person or persons but to Hugh Yeadall, receiving only of him for the title of the said tenement 40/-, and a mazer and a silver spoon, with a lead and other implements there. And if the said Nicholas be dead then I will that the mother of the said Nicholas and such children as she hath in full life begotten by Richard Pepper and her shall have forty pounds of the said hundred marks, and the rest to be at the order and disposition of my executors to the performance of this my present last will and testament. Also if the said Nicholas die then I bequeath the abbey field sheep close and deeding in manner and upon like condition as before, and for the rent paying, to John Chachirde and William Pepper. Also I bequeath to master Thomas Hardwick of Potter Newton and to John Moore the King's Majesty's servant the third part of such ground as I have in lease at Cookridge, the third part whereof is £6, either of them yearly to pay £3 during the years which I have in it to come. Also I bequeath to Thomas Yeadall and Richard Wood* the other two parts, either of them paying yearly for the same £6. Also I bequeath to Sir Anthony Jackson* and his mother a parcel of ground in Cookridge late in the holding of Robert Cookson, for the rent paying which is 18/-, for all the space abovesaid. Also I give to his mother one quarter of wheat. Also I bequeath to every godchild that I have one lamb, and to Sir Leonard Wyndresse* a camlet jacket. Also I bequeath to William Archdale my servant my grey nag, my saddle, my bridle, my boots, my spurs, my doublet, my hose, my shoes, a mattress, a pair of sheets, a pair of blankets, two coverlets and forty shillings in money. Also I bequeath to mistress Paginam my white gelding, and to her and to her children, so that she do seal one general acquittance to my executors, £20 which my master Paginam doth owe me, that is to wit £10 and £10 to her children. Also I bequeath to Mr. Woodforth my gelding called 'Schaghe'. Also I bequeath to John Scatcherd and William Pepper, either of them 40/-. Also I bequeath to Margaret Wade 10/-, and to Anne Judson and Janet Typling, either of them 6/8. Also I bequeath to Sir William Lupton* one feather bed and one bolster and my best gown. Also I will that every house in Adel parish, at discretion of mine executors, have one bushel of rye, and every house in Adel and the Smithies two bushels. Also William Cook, Thomas Thornton, Dogeson's wife, Archdale's wife, Alexander Browne, every one two bushels of rye. Also I will that my executors shall at their discretion distribute to poor folks of Bramley two quarters of rye. Also I will that they distribute within the township of Headingley at their discretion twelve bushles of rye. Also I will that Emma Farrow have my years unspent of my lease which I have of the Sand Beds. Also I will that Thomas Yeadall shall have 20 couples of my best ewes and lambs at Cookridge. Also I will that he have to the use of his three children the herbage and pannage of Weetwood upon condition that the tenants of the Smithies have yearly the pasturing of four horses without anything paying therefor in the west part of the same betwixt May day and the feast of St. Michael during the term of my years thereof, the said Thomas Yeadall paying yearly for the same 40/-. Also I give to Thomas Yeadall, for the farm paying, my term of years which I have in the Kirkgarths with the appurtenances, and the Kitchengarths with like appurtenances, and also such feesing as is now in my occupation at Kirkstall, expressed in a lease bearing date the (blank) day of (blank) in the year of our sovereign lord Edward the sixth. Also I give to the said Thomas and his wife one cupboard, one counter and round table in my chamber, with 2 feather beds with bolsters, three pair of my best sheets, three pair of blankets, with hangings and bedstocks of my own bed, with a overse covering the best, and a counter cloth with five silver spoons. Also I give to Thomas Dolif of Bramley one girdle which was my mother's. Also I give to William Pepper, brother to the said Nicholas, 20/- of money and one of my best coal horses and a coat, if he be in full life and come down for them. Also I do release to Peter Casson and Christopher Garret in yearly rent for the Long Holme 23/4 upon condition that they do pay 20/- to Richard Hollings of Horsforth which I give unto him. Also I do release unto Thomas Willey and Thomas Naylor for every bloom at the blowing at the Smithies 8*d*. upon condition they or their assigns do perform fulfil all manner of covenants and payments specified by indenture betwixt them and me without coven fraud or deceit as my executors shall see that they do. Also I will that my executors shall pay the one half or moiety to be taken for every bloom, that is to wit 8*d*. for every bloom, by the space of one whole year to (blank) Newson, wife to (blank) Newson of Weeton, and Wigan, wife to Robert Wigan, and the other half, that is to say other 8*d*. that year, and the whole sum of 16*d*. yearly to be after that distributed to the poor folks of Adel and other places at the discretion of my executors, so long as the said endureth. Also I give to Robert (blank) my servant 6/8. Also I bequeath to Mr. Thomas Hardwick of Potter Newton, and John Moore servant to the King's Majesty, either of them, five marks over and besides all manner of costs and charges to be sustained by them for me in every behalf concerning the performance of this my present last will and testament, to be had taken and preserved of my whole goods and debts owing to me, whom I do make my executors of the same, and Mr. Anthony Crane of London to be adjoined to them. And also I give to him five pounds over and besides costs and charges, to be allowed as above. THE RESIDUE of all my goods movable and immovable and debts owing to me I give to them to dispose and order to the poor and highways for my soul's health, at their discretion, their own pains to be considered. Also I make Mr. Thomas Stadeven one of the supervisors of this my present will and I give unto him 10 angels of gold, and my godfather Sir Anthony Jackson* the other supervisor, to whom I give a jacket of caffa, they to give their advice and counsel to my said executors when they are required so to do, and their costs and charges to be borne by my said executors from time to time. Also I give to Thomas Wroose my best pair of shears, and to John Askwith the other pair. Also I will that seven pounds which Mr. Gilbert Leigh doth owe me be perceived and taken by my executors and to be bestowed upon mending of highways nigh Leeds, whereas I have informed my executors. IN WITNESS whereof I have subscribed this my present will and testament with my own hand the year and day abovesaid, these being witnesses, Robert Judson, Peter Casson, Nicholas Kent, and other more.

NONO DIE MENSIS junii anno domini millesimo quingensimo liij° probatum fuit hoc presens Testamentum dicti defuncti, etc.

2. The Will of Joan Harkay, Late Prioress of Ellerton

(From *Wills and Inventories from the registry of the Archdeaconry of Richmond, 1442–1579*, edited by J. Raine, Surtees Society, vol. 26. The spelling has been modernised and punctuation supplied. Amounts given in figures have been converted from Roman to Arabic numerals. The four names marked * are those of former nuns of Ellerton. The Sir Gabriel Lofthouse among the beneficiaries is a former monk of Kirkstall who had a chaplaincy in Richmond. For commentary see above, p. 156.)

In Dei nomine, Amen. In the year of our Lord God 1550, the eighth day of April, I dame Joan Harkay of Richmond, knowing me mortal, being of no certainty of the hour of my death, therefore willing to provide for the health of my soul and discharge of my conscience, of whole mind, maketh ordain and declareth my last will and testament after this form following. First I give my soul unto Almighty God and our Lady Saint Mary, and to all the Saints in heaven, to pray for me, and my bones to be buried in the church of Richmond of our Lady side. Item I give for my mortuary according to the King's acts. Item I give to every priest dwelling in Richmond 6*d.* to pray for me at my burial, and priests without town that cometh to my burial 4*d.* Item I give to four widows 2*d.* apiece to watch to the time that my body be buried, and to pray for me. Item I give to Margaret Symson a ring of gold. Item I give to Janet Hutchesson of Ruckthroft 20*d.* Item I give to Janet Symson 20*d.* Item I give to four of my sisters, dame Alice Tomson*, dame Cecilia Swale*, dame Agnes Aslayby*, dame Elizabeth Parker*, 12*d.* apiece. Item I give to Anthony Metcalf 20*d.* Item I give to Cecilia Wilson 20*d.* Item I give to John Atkinson 12*d.* Item I given to Isabel Coulling and Isabel Heighington Anne of Moore and Henry Nelson's wife, to every of them a kerchief. Item I give to Sir John Moore, Sir Gabriel Lofthouse 12*d*. apiece. Item I give to Sir Cuthbert Hutchesson and Sir William Lofthouse 20*d*. apiece. Item I give to Christopher Harkay's son 20*d*. Item I give to Cecil Conyers a silver spoon, and to his daughter Emma a spruce coffer. Item I give to Giles and John his sons 12*d*. apiece. Item I give to Jeffrey Ward and his two sons 2/-. Item I make and ordain dame Margaret Dowson my executrix, if the law will suffer her, and if the law will not suffer her to be my executrix, then I will that William Dowson be my executor to order and fulfil this my last will and testament according to my mind. Item I give to my executrix dame Margaret Dowson, or to William Dowson my executor, the residue of my goods, my debts paid and legacies fulfilled, to dispose further as she shall think good for the health of my soul, if any can be spared, at the oversight of Sir Cuthbert Hutchesson and Sir William Lofthouse. These being witnesses, Sir Ralph Lynnwraye, Richard Binks, Ralph Coulling, Arthur Johnson, Sir Cuthbert Hutchesson and Sir William Lofthouse, cum multis aliis.

This is the true INVENTORY of all the goods movable and immovable of dame Joan Harkay, praised by four honest men, Richard Binks, Ralph Lynnwraye, Francis Nelson and Edward Satterwait.

Inprimis one brass pot	3/–
Item one other brass pot	18*d*.
Item two pans	2/–
Item one frying pan and one roast iron	8*d*.
Item two pewter dishes with two pewter saucers and one pewter basin	2/–
Item one ewer	3/4
Item two little chests with a coffer	2/8
Item one chair	8*d*.
Item tongs and racking crook	8*d*.
Item 3 cushions	18*d*.
Item one evil feather bed with all things thereto belonging	20/–
Item a kirtle and a coat with other linen gear	10/–
Item old painted cloths	12*d*.
Item in ready money	20/–
Item one aumbrey	3/4
Summa Totalis	£3 : 12 : 4

11

The Consequences

MANY writers in the past have chosen to regard the dissolution of the monasteries as one of the most important events in the Tudor period, or indeed in the whole of England's history, and have attributed to it revolutionary political, social, religious or economic results. Some have stressed the importance of the suppression in ensuring the permanence of the English reformation by creating among the lay recipients of monastic estates a vested interest in the repudiation of papal claims. Others have seen, as its principal consequence, the creation of a new landed class whose ambition for political power commensurate with their economic led in the next century to the overthrow of royal government and the establishment of a parliamentary monarchy. Others have chosen to regard the destruction of the abbeys as the end of a medieval age of piety when the charitable mantle of the church covered and protected the ailing and unfortunate, and the beginning of a modern age of naked commercialism when poverty and unemployment first become nationwide problems. Yet others have hailed, with the disappearance of the regular orders, the passing of an era of obscurantism and superstition and the dawning of a new age of light and reason. There is some truth in each of these views, but none of them expresses the whole truth, and each tends to one degree or another to exaggerate the extent of the connection between the dissolution and the consequence it claims sprang from it.

The Political Consequences

It is of course beyond question that those who purchased monastic estates in good faith and for good money, and this means the great majority of the purchasers, were unlikely to treat with any enthusiasm any suggestion that the religious orders should be restored. To Queen Mary's appeals they turned deaf ears. Her lead in refounding Westminster, Greenwich, Sheen, Smithfield, Syon and Dartford, by the return to these communities of buildings and estates still in the possession of the crown, was, not surprisingly, not followed by any private benefactors, who preferred to keep what they had bought. The restoration of catholicism and the papal supremacy in Mary's reign was hedged about with qualifications. Cardinal Pole, very much against his will, had, in response to parliamentary pressures, to confirm in their possession of former abbey lands all who had secured any such by grant or purchase, and this concession by the cardinal legate was later endorsed by pope Julius III in June 1555 by the bull *Praeclara*. All this must be readily conceded.

And yet, as we have already pointed out in Chapter 9, the steadfast opposition of Mary's parliaments to any proposal for a general restoration of the religious orders was less a matter of protestant prejudice than of simple common sense. It was not the secularisation and dispersal of the monastic lands that made England a protestant nation. It did not prevent, or even make particularly difficult, the reacceptance under Mary of the pope and the Latin mass. A catholic, but monastery-free England was perfectly possible, and might indeed have emerged in the sixteenth century had Mary lived longer or borne an heir.

In the seventeenth century, however, when catholicism had acquired, through the widespread dissemination of John Foxe's *Acts and Monuments*, an evil repute in England, and when the temporary triumph of the catholic forces in the early stages of the Thirty Years' War had led to the forcible restoration of secularised church lands in Germany by the Imperial Edict of Restitution of 1629, Englishmen began to see a closer association between the claims of the papacy and the ownership of the abbey lands, and to regard any move towards a reconciliation with Rome as a threat to the 'settlement of property' in the kingdom. By the reign of Charles II a vested interest in protestantism had more clearly emerged, and was to contribute substantially to the persistence right into the nineteenth century of political discrimination against Roman Catholics in England. But it was not the dissolution alone which had created this interest, nor is there very much sign of it in the sixteenth century when there is indeed little evidence of any direct connection between the possession of monastic lands and the profession of protestant sentiments. The rise of puritanism, the real foundation of English protestantism, owes no direct debt to the dissolution of the monasteries.

The influence of the suppression in creating a new and politically ambitious landed class has also, as we have seen in Chapter 9, been exaggerated. The emergence of the gentry as the dominant class may to a certain extent have been assisted by their acquisition of additional acres in the 1540s and later, but more important than the fact of their purchases were the economic pressures which obliged the crown to sell. The war expenditure of Henry VIII and Elizabeth I, coupled with the steady inflation of the sixteenth century, progressively eroded the financial resources of the monarchy and made it impossible, by the time of James I, for the king to 'live of his own' even in time of peace. The predominance of the gentry in the house of commons and the control over taxation exercised by that body, which then came into play and provided the landed classes with the opportunity to further their political ambitions, were neither of them new features of the parliamentary scene. They both can be traced back well beyond the decade of the dissolution. Indeed it could be argued that the transfer to the crown of the monastic estates delayed rather than accelerated the emergence of the gentry as a political force by deferring the day when the crown's financial dependence upon parliamentary grants would give them their chance.

There were also other influences at work in the sixteenth century which should not be overlooked; the spread of secular education, creating a new self-confidence among the laity and developing in them an active interest in national and international affairs; the long reign of a woman in a still male-dominated society; the effective and permanent curbing of the powers of the ancient nobility who so often in times past had dominated the political scene; the establishment of internal peace and good government which, releasing men from the need to concentrate primarily on self-defence, gave rein to their ambition; these, and other related developments, played their part in the rise of the gentry to political predominance. To attribute this rise solely, or even largely, to the dispersal among the laity of the monastic lands is to distort the truth by over-simplification.

The Social Consequences

Those who claim that the destruction of the religious houses involved the destruction of the extensive social services which they supplied and so brought considerable hardship in its train, frequently also claim that the change in ownership of the monastic estates led to an acceleration of enclosures and to a significant increase in rural un-employment. These two closely associated points are best dealt with together. The extent of the social services provided by the religious orders we have already discussed in some detail in Chapter 2. We saw there, for instance, that the contribution of the monks and nuns to education was not very significant as they were concerned mainly with the teaching of their own novices and postulates. The universities, of course, lost some students when the houses of study maintained by the religious orders at Oxford and Cambridge were closed down, but the numbers lost were soon more than made up by the influx of the sons of the gentry for whom a sojourn at the university, if not an actual degree, was rapidly becoming an essential part of their education. At the same time the number of schools and colleges to which the gentry could send their sons was being steadily increased by new foundations. The sixteenth century is a notable one for the endowment of grammar schools and Oxford and Cambridge colleges. Many of these, it is true, rose, like Fisher's St. John's, Wolsey's Cardinal College, Audley's Magdalene and Mildmay's Emmanuel, on the remains of former religious houses, and some were established by men who had profited from the dissolution, but as a general rule the connection between the disappearance of the religious orders and the appearance of the new educational establishments is fortuitous rather than significant. Indeed this expansion of educational facilities had begun in the fifteenth century, and was to carry on into the seventeenth. Kings and bishops were the earliest founders, the participation of the lesser ranks of the laity in the movement comes rather later, but more as part of the general secularisation of society than as a specific consequence of the suppression of the religious orders. The school-founding habit of post-dissolution years is merely the continuation of a pre-dissolution movement. There was no newly-created 'educational gap' for the Elizabethan founders to fill.

We also observed in Chapter 2 that on the whole the ancient tradition of hospitality was well maintained by the religious orders, and, in Chapter 5, that the dissolution act required, under penalty, that the new owners of monastic properties should keep these standards up. This part of the act was, however, largely ineffective, and the 'decay of hospitality' was almost as frequently remarked upon by contemporaries as the decay of tillage. Yet this falling off in the standards of hospitality was not necessarily a specific consequence of the dissolution. The entertaining of travellers had never been the exclusive monopoly of the religious orders, but was an obligation which rested upon all persons of substance, and it was a point of pride with the great noble that he never turned any genuine wayfarer away from his doors. But the pressure of inflation was inexorable and many nobles and gentry were obliged to become rather more selective in their entertaining. Their friends and social equals they would continue, as before, to feast as lavishly as they could afford, but the casual traveller, the humble itinerant, might well find himself rather less welcome at the great man's board. Whether his host lived in a former abbey or not was quite irrelevant. All were subject to the same pressures, and the decay of hospitality was a general phenomenon which cannot be shown to have resulted directly from the suppression.

The precise extent and nature of the connection between the dissolution and the problem of poor relief is not so easily determined. As we saw in Chapter 2, we are in no position to make categoric statements about the value or extent of monastic charity. It may have been extensive and made quite an important contribution to the relief of distress. It may have been limited to the obligatory doles and have hardly touched the problem at all. It is therefore clearly impossible to assess with any certainty how seriously the dissolution aggravated the problem of poverty by depriving the unfortunate of the aid and comfort of the religious houses.

On the other hand we can be quite clear about one point, namely that the problem of vagrancy was not suddenly created by the dissolution, but had already attained serious proportions even before the suppression began. One of the first acts of parliament to attempt to deal with the matter was the Act for the punishment of Beggars and Vagabonds (22 Henry VIII, c. 12), passed in 1531, which established the important distinction between those who could not and those who would not work, though it offered no help to the former but a licence to beg locally. The sturdy beggar was already a familiar figure on the roads of England five years before the dissolution act was passed. Vagabondage was the product of many causes; the pressure of an expanding population upon a limited supply of cultivated land; the continuing tendency towards the conversion of arable acres into pasture to meet the apparently insatiable demands of an expanding cloth manufacture; the raising of rents by landlords struggling to keep pace with rising costs; the cutting down of the size of noble households as a measure of economy in an age of inflation; to name but four, and these causes were largely independent of the fate of the religious houses. Monastic landlords were just as ready as their lay equivalents to enclose, or to push up rents, and the change in ownership of the abbey lands did not, as we saw in Chapter 1, make any significant difference to the way in which they were administered.

Monastic Servants

But even if the dissolution did not result in the sudden eviction of hordes of monastic tenants, could it not have added significantly to the pool of unemployed by putting out of work large numbers of monastic servants and domestic employees whose services the new owners might well not need? It is, after all, quite clear from the Suppression Papers that the number of persons directly employed by the religious in and about the cloister was quite extensive. Even the eight nuns in the little house at Handale had a domestic staff of six; a butler, a cook, two maidservants and two boys (Chapter 6, Appendix). The domestics at some of the larger abbeys were numbered in scores, and at the dissolution they were, as a general rule, dismissed with a quarter's wages in their hands. How many were re-employed by the new owners we cannot tell.

It is indeed only very occasionally that we come across any reference to the fate of individual abbey servants. This is only natural for people of their rank in society did not very frequently in that age leave any trace of their names in contemporary records, and when they did, the fact that some of them had at one time been employed by monks or nuns would not always be considered worthy of note. In only one class of records, that arising from post-dissolution litigation over abbey lands, their extent and location and the rights and privileges attaching to ownership of them, are abbey servants regularly named as such. When summoned to bear witness to pre-dissolution practices it was very important that the nature and length of their association with the abbey in question should be made quite plain. From such records we do, therefore, get occasional glimpses of former monastic employees, but it is arguable that the picture we get is somewhat distorted. In the first place the incidence of such records of post-dissolution litigation is quite irregular, and depends upon the existence of some dispute considered by the parties concerned to be worth taking to court. In the second place, when former servants were called to give evidence those who still lived in the vicinity of the dissolved abbey were more likely to be chosen because they were the more easily traceable. In the third place, because the testimony of a man of modest substance was usually preferred to that of a pauper, it is generally the more fortunate of the ex-employees of the abbey who feature in the record. Our sample of former servants is therefore random, but weighted, weighted in favour of those who found satisfactory alternative employment near at hand. Those who were thrown on the roads or who took to vagrancy were not likely to be summoned to give testimony in court.

A good example, both of this inbuilt prejudice of the sources and of the overall inadequacy of our knowledge of the fate of monastic servants, is provided by the priory of Monk Bretton. A series of lawsuits in the reign of Elizabeth I supplies us incidentally with information about seven former employees of the prior and convent. Three of them, each with between fourteen and sixteen years of service to the priory before its dissolution, had lived on afterwards in Monk Bretton itself, and were still there in 1574. All three were then described as husbandmen, and two were said to be worth twenty nobles apiece. Three others, one of them formerly employed as a brewer by the monks, another having had charge of the priory's horses, still lived within a two mile radius of Monk Bretton. They were said to be worth twenty nobles, thirty pounds and twenty marks respectively. The seventh, who lived farthest away, was three miles off, at Silkstone. Though in former days he had acted as overseer of all the priory's granges he had since fallen on hard times and, aged 80 at the time of giving his evidence, 'valet nihil in bonis'.

These notices of seven of the former servants at Monk Bretton can be supplemented by references to three others whose sons were still living within a few miles of the priory in 1590 and 1601, and who had presumably therefore found work in the neighbourhood after the dissolution. This brings the total number of servants about whom we know anything at all to ten, which is less than a quarter of the forty-seven who served the priory in the year of its dissolution. When it is remembered that the former servants of this particular priory are better documented than most, we can see how difficult it is to judge the general effect of the suppression upon the fortunes of this particular section of the population.

To some abbey servants the dissolution clearly made little difference. We must remember that the new owner took over the monastic site and demesnes as a going concern, and that, unless he wished to introduce sweeping changes in the management and working of that concern, there would be substantial continuity of employment for the agricultural labour force. For the domestic staff the prospects were less promising unless the new occupant intended to make the abbey his principal residence. Even then he might not need as large a staff as his predecessors the monks. There must have been some unemployment and some distress, but we have no effective means of measuring how much. Contemporary references to 'Abbey Lubbers' (a term which is rather imprecise and may include not only those who depended for a living upon monastic doles but also those who had formerly found honest employment in the religious houses) which suggest that they formed an important constituent of the bands of roving beggars, are too subjective and rhetorical to be precise. On the other hand, because of the extent of our ignorance of individual cases, we cannot blandly deny that the dissolution caused any additional distress. Undoubtedly the disappearance of the monasteries, both as employers of labour and as relievers of the poor, had its specific contribution to make to the twin problems of poverty and unemployment, but, quite independently of the fate of the religious orders, these problems were, for other reasons, already at that time becoming acute.

Some further distress may have been caused among the elderly by the fact that such retirement benefits as corrodies and annuities were no longer available for purchase, but, taken all in all, the social consequences of the dissolution would appear to have been marginal rather than revolutionary.

The Intellectual Consequences

The same is in general true of the intellectual consequences. Although they tended on the whole to be conservative in outlook, the religious orders were not by any means sunk in barbarous ignorance. We have already observed the care for their books displayed by the monks of Monk Bretton (above, pp. 152–3). A group of private letters written by a monk of Evesham in the years 1528–31 reveals to us the extent to which the literary studies of the great humanists of his day had caught his imagination and that of his many correspondents, a high proportion of whom were also monks in other houses. In yet other convents the leaven of Lutheranism was at work, as can be seen in its later fruits; John Hooper, Edwardian bishop of Gloucester, and often cast in the role of 'the first English Puritan', was at one time a Cistercian monk; William Barlow, the reforming Henrician bishop of St. David's, began his ecclesiastical career as an Augustinian canon; Miles Coverdale, translator and editor of the English Bible, was a former Austin friar, as was also Robert Barnes who was a notable protestant propagandist in the 1530s. These are some of the better-known ex-regulars turned reformers, but there were many others less famous who were equally influenced by the intellectual currents of their generation. Membership of a religious order did not inhibit a man's intellectual curiosity, nor necessarily mould his mind in a conservative cast. On the contrary it might well provide him with opportunities for study which he might not otherwise have had. The monasteries were not barriers in the way of intellectual advance. It was not necessary that they should be swept away before the 'new learning' could triumph. This intellectual movement gained its converts freely both within and outside the cloister, and its advance was neither significantly aided nor hindered by the dissolution.

There was, however, one less direct way in which the suppression of the religious orders affected the contemporary intellectual climate and materially assisted the cause of the reformers. The association between monasteries and prayers for the dead was quite clear to most Englishmen of the reign of Henry VIII, whatever their intellectual abilities or social status. The prime duty incumbent upon any monastic community was to maintain the daily round of services and intercessions both for the living and for the dead, but especially for the latter, and of the latter especially the founder and other benefactors of the house itself. To suppress the monasteries without making any provision for continuing this service of prayer was to imply that such intercessions had no specific efficacy, and to suggest that the souls of deceased benefactors would suffer no spiritual loss as a result of their being discontinued. Thus the dissolution, by implication, undermined the contemporary teaching of the church about purgatory and the ability of the living to assist with their prayers the souls of the departed, and was, to this extent, a concession to the disciples of Luther.

Only a few years before the fall of the monasteries Simon Fish and Sir Thomas More had argued this very point in public, in pamphlet form. Fish's *Supplication for the Beggars* had suggested that the religious orders were parasites upon the nation, taking much and giving nothing in return. More had written in reply, in his *Supplication for Souls*, a fervent appeal for the souls in torment whose suffering was daily alleviated by the prayers of the monks. Latimer, a few years later, put the matter very pithily in a short treatise which he prepared for king Henry himself:

> 'The founding of monasteries argued purgatory to be, so the putting of them down argueth it not to be.'

Purgatory was clearly at issue in the dissolution, and pilgrimages and relics also, as we noted in Chapter 4, came under attack at the same time. Thus, by turning against the religious orders, the government, whatever its real intentions may have been, appeared to be taking sides with the reformers against these particular aspects of contemporary orthodoxy. The Henrician church was not merely 'Catholicism without the Pope' but also 'Catholicism without pilgrimages, relics or religious orders', and so had taken more than one significant step in the direction of Lutheranism. This naturally gave Lutheran sympathisers in England encouragement and grounds for hope, and correspondingly discouraged the conservatives. The suppression of the religious houses, and of the practices so intimately associated with them, significantly altered the accepted pattern of piety and observance and prepared the minds of the people for subsequent changes of a much more radical nature.

The Secularisation of Society

The dissolution also had its contribution to make to the reduction in the numbers of the clergy, and so to the general secularisation of society which is so prominent a feature of English history in the sixteenth century, but it would perhaps be truer to say that the disappearance of the religious orders was more a symptom of that secularisation than a significant contributory cause. The ease with which the religious were dispersed and their property applied to secular purposes, and the comparative readiness of the monks, canons, nuns and friars, and their former tenants and neighbours, to adjust themselves smoothly to the new conditions of life, suggest strongly that monasticism on the medieval scale was no longer meeting any widespread vital spiritual or social need, and that a radical pruning operation upon an overgrown and not very vigorous institution was long overdue. Whether it was right or necessary to uproot the plant altogether is quite another question.

M

Bibliographical Note

THE most sympathetic modern account of the dissolution of the monasteries is that contained in M. D. Knowles' great classic *The Religious Orders in England*, vol. III, part iii (Cambridge University Press, 1961), which has quite superseded Cardinal Gasquet's pioneer, but not wholly reliable, *Henry VIII and the English Monasteries* (John Hodges, 1888–9) as the standard Catholic work. Those who still wish to read Gasquet should first read Knowles' essay on *Cardinal Gasquet as an Historian* (Athlone Press, 1957) and exercise the appropriate caution. G. Baskerville's *English Monks and the Suppression of the Monasteries* (Jonathan Cape, 1937) provided a useful corrective to Gasquet, but was altogether too optimistic.

In recent decades a considerable amount of detailed work has been done on the effects of the dissolution on (*a*) the lives of the former religious and (*b*) the market for and tenure of landed property. The results of these labours are to be found in articles in the learned journals, of which the following are the most worthy of note:

(*a*) Baskerville, G. 'The Dispossessed Religious of Gloucestershire,' in *Transactions of the Bristol and Gloucestershire Archaeological Society*, vol. XLIX, 1927.
—— 'The Married Clergy and Pensioned Religious in the Norwich Diocese', in *English Historical Review*, vol. XLVIII, 1933.
—— 'The Dispossessed Religious in Surrey', in *Surrey Archaeological Collections*, vol. XLVII, 1941.
Dickens, A. G. 'The Edwardian arrears in Augmentations Payments,' in *English Historical Review*, vol. LV, 1940.
(*b*) Habakkuk, H. J. 'The Market for Monastic Property', in *Economic History Review*, 2nd series, vol. X, 1958.
Youings, J. 'The Terms of the Disposal of the Devon Monastic Lands', in *English Historical Review*, vol. LXIX, 1954.

A number of local studies are also available, of which the following are the most important:

Archbold, W. A. J. *The Somerset Religious Houses* (Cambridge, 1892).

Councer, C. R. 'The Dissolution of the Kentish Monasteries', in *Archaeologia Cantiana*, vol. XLVII, 1935.

Hay, D. 'The Dissolution of the Monasteries in the Diocese of Durham', in *Archaeologia Aeliana*, 4th series, vol. XV, 1938.

Hibbert, F. A. *The Dissolution of the Monasteries* (in Staffordshire), London, 1910.

Hodgett, G. A. J. 'The Dissolution of the Religious Houses in Lincolnshire', in *Lincolnshire Architectural and Archaeological Society's Reports and Papers*, 4th series, part i, 1951.

Those who wish to follow up the history of the dissolution in their own area will find the following invaluable:

Knowles, M. D. and Hadcock, R. N. *Medieval Religious Houses* (Longmans 1953) for the location and identification of the sites.

The appropriate volumes of the *Victoria County History* for brief accounts of every abbey.

The *Valor Ecclesiasticus* (Record Commission edition, 1810–34) for the economy of the religious houses.

Savine, A. *English Monasteries on the Eve of the Dissolution* (Oxford Studies in Social and Legal History, vol. 1, 1909) as a guide to the interpretation of the *Valor*.

The Calendar of Letters and Papers of the Reign of Henry VIII, especially vols. IX to XV, for a medley of documents relating to the dissolution: visitors' comments, deeds of surrender, pension lists, summaries of augmentations accounts, etc.

The publications of local Archaeological and Record societies can generally be relied upon to contain a good deal of material on the local abbeys.

Index